W9-ANH-800

WOMEN'S
DAILY
DECLARATIONS
FOR SPIRITUAL
WARFARE

WOMEN'S DAILY DECLARATIONS FOR SPIRITUAL WARFARE

JOHN ECKHARDT

CHARISMA
HOUSE

Most CHARISMA HOUSE BOOK GROUP products are available at special quantity discounts for bulk purchase for sales promotions, premiums, fund-raising, and educational needs. For details, write Charisma House Book Group, 600 Rinehart Road, Lake Mary, Florida 32746, or telephone (407) 333-0600.

WOMEN'S DAILY DECLARATIONS FOR SPIRITUAL WARFARE
    by John Eckhardt
Published by Charisma House
Charisma Media/Charisma House Book Group
600 Rinehart Road
Lake Mary, Florida 32746
www.charismahouse.com

Cover design by Justin Evans
Design Director: Bill Johnson

Visit the author's website at www.impactnetwork.net.

Library of Congress Cataloging-in-Publication Data
An application to register this book for cataloging has been submitted to the Library of Congress.
International Standard Book Number: 978-1-62136-299-9
E-book ISBN: 978-1-62136-518-1

Portions of this book were previously published as *Daily Declarations for Spiritual Warfare* by Charisma House, ISBN 978-1-61638-443-2, copyright © 2011.

This publication has been translated in Spanish under the title *Declaraciones diarias de guerra espiritual para la mujer*, copyright © 2013 by John Eckhardt, published by Casa Creación, a Charisma Media company. All rights reserved.

13 14 15 16 17 — 9 8 7 6 5 4 3 2 1
Printed in the United States of America

INTRODUCTION

THE MOST IMPORTANT reasons we were given the Bible—*the Word of God*—are so that we can know the wonderful plans that God has for us, experience His presence in our lives, and be equipped to fulfill His will on earth.

The Bible contains God's words—the specific things He knew we would need to know in order to live a life that pleases Him. He wants us to hear His voice in our spirits no matter what the circumstances are in life or how many other voices are pressing upon us for our attention. His voice rises above the din and confusion of all other sounds—if we have learned to listen for His voice and to recognize Him when He is speaking to us.

God's presence in our lives and His words within our spirit can dispel the greatest sorrow, cut through the clouds of distraction and confusion, and rise above the threats and taunts of demonic spirits that would bind us to their evil, godless philosophies and snatch us from God's promise of eternity with Him.

But God's Word cannot do any of these things unless we have diligently studied His written Word and learned to recognize His voice of revelation speaking in our spirits. It cannot guide us on the path of righteousness or keep us out of the captivity of Satan unless we know it. It will not instruct in spiritual warfare in our battles with Satan and his demonic forces unless it has become our warfare victory manual.

This book is filled with God's words for us today. It is written in His voice, and reading it will be like sitting at His feet as He speaks to us about our daily interactions and needs. It seeks to articulate the thoughts of God for His daughters. It will inform your day, guide your path, strengthen your resolve, and provide your defensive strategies against Satan.

God Himself spoke to us about the importance of knowing and hearing His Words when He said:

> "My thoughts are not your thoughts,
>   neither are your ways my ways," declares
>   the Lord.
> "As the heavens are higher than the earth,
>   so are my ways higher than your ways
>   and my thoughts than your thoughts.
> As the rain and the snow
>   come down from heaven,
> and do not return to it
>   without watering the earth
> and making it bud and flourish,
>   so that it yields seed for the sower and
>   bread for the eater,
> so is my word that goes out from my mouth:
>   It will not return to me empty,
> but will accomplish what I desire
>   and achieve the purpose for which I sent it."
>   —Isaiah 55:8–11, niv

Use this book to allow God to sit with you in conversation each day, and to fill your spirit with His counsel and guidance. It will enrich your life and prepare you to be victorious in each circumstance and situation that you face. God's Word—whether written or whispered silently in your spirit—will be all you need to live a life that is fully pleasing to Him.

JANUARY

Meeting With Your Commander

MY WORD AND MY POWER ARE ALL YOU NEED

IN MY WORD you will discover the thoughts that I think about you. I have desired that your life be filled with My great peace, not with the evil and turmoil that you will find in the world, which the enemy will try to thrust upon you. My Word will help you to see the glorious future I have planned for you and will surround your life with the hope of overcoming the evil in this world through My strength and power. Allow My Holy Spirit to fill you up with My supernatural power. With My power there is nothing the enemy can do to hurt you, My daughter. My Word and My power will help you to fill the whole earth with My glory.

JEREMIAH 29:11; MATTHEW 10:1; PSALM 72:19

Prayer Declaration

Father, Your Word tells me to call to You, and You will answer me and show me great and mighty things, which I do not know. I am calling to You today!

I LONG TO MEET WITH YOU

MY DAUGHTER, I long to spend time with you every day. If you will only call to Me, I will answer you and show you great and mighty things that I can do for you, things that you do not know. I delight in the prayers you pray to Me. My ears are continually open to hear you call to Me. Your earnest and heartfelt prayers will cause My tremendous power to be available to you. Learn to pray without ceasing, and I will bring you salvation and deliverance from your enemies. The enemy wants to cause you to be powerless and hopeless in this present day. But I am Your Helper, and I will not despise your prayer or turn away from you. If you will only meet with Me every day, I will give you My Spirit's power to overcome the enemy.

JEREMIAH 33:3; JAMES 5:16, AMP; PSALMS 18:3; 66:20

Prayer Declaration

Lord, I waited patiently for You, and You heard my cry. You lifted me out of a slimy pit of mud and mire, and You set my feet firmly on a rock. You put a new song in my mouth and gave me a hymn of praise I can sing to You. Let those around me see and learn to put their trust also in You.

I WANT YOU TO USE MY WORDS TO SET THE CAPTIVES FREE

IF YOU WILL confess My Word daily and meet with Me in prayer daily, I will give you a great release of My power in your life. My Spirit will illuminate My Word to you and help you to see clearly My plan for your life—and how the enemy wants to stop that plan! As you read My Word and meet with Me through prayer, your faith will keep you from becoming sluggish and dull spiritually, and because of your faith, you will inherit My promises. Remember My servant Daniel, who was able to pray effectively because he knew My Word concerning My people. Today many of My daughters are held captive by the evil, sinful desires of people who are controlled by the enemy. When you pray and confess My Word, you will be able to release My mind, which brings My Spirit and My life to those in bondage.

ISAIAH 33:2; HEBREWS 6:11–12; JOHN 6:63

Prayer Declaration

Father, Your Holy Spirit has illuminated Your Word to me and given me weapons of warfare that are filled with Your power, which I am using daily to wage war against the enemy and to demolish strongholds.

I WANT TO GIVE YOU THE KEYS TO MY KINGDOM

HAVE YOU BECOME disillusioned and discouraged because of the wickedness and corruption that exist all around you in this sinful world? Don't you know that I want to give you the keys to My kingdom in heaven? Not even hell itself will be able to prevail against My kingdom. With the keys to My kingdom, I have given you authority to bind and loose. You will be able to restrict, stop, hinder, fetter, check, hold back, arrest, and put a stop to the demonic strongholds in your world. You can use the keys of My kingdom to lock up sickness and disease, hurt, witchcraft, poverty, death, destruction, confusion, defeat, and discouragement from your life. By doing that you will loose yourself—and others—from the works of darkness, the works of Satan. Always remember that I have given My daughters—you—power and authority over all devils.

MATTHEW 16:19; 10:1

Prayer Declaration

You have promised, Lord, that the effectual fervent prayer of a righteous woman is powerful. You take delight in answering me when I call, and You are doing great and mighty things in my life.

My Word Will Give You Power to Demolish Strongholds

As you continue to take a stand on the promises I have given you in My Word, you will be able to demolish the satanic strongholds around you. My Word is more powerful than the raging fires that cause destruction and death wherever they rage. My Word is a strong fire that will burn up the works of wickedness. Do you hate every false way that Satan uses to sidetrack people from the path of life onto the path of death? Do you want to see changes in your city, region, and nation? I have given you the power to represent My kingdom and to even change geographic regions. You, My daughter, are a king in My kingdom, and your word is filled with authority and power against the kingdoms of this evil world. Stand firm in the power I have given you. Don't suffer unnecessarily by failing to exercise your authority in Me.

Psalm 119:104; Jeremiah 23:29

Prayer Declaration

*O God, I will use Your Word like a powerful
hammer to break down all of Satan's defensive borders.
Your Word will spread like a wild fire throughout the
enemy's domain, burning up all his works of darkness.*

MY POWER WILL MAKE YOU VICTORIOUS

ALWAYS REMEMBER THAT you are not wrestling against flesh and blood. If you want to overcome and be victorious over principalities and powers, learn to prepare yourself in My armor. Buckle My belt of truth around your waist, and put on My breastplate of righteousness. Fit your feet with the readiness that comes from the gospel of peace. As you prepare to move forward into battle with Satan and his demonic forces, take up the shield of faith, for it will extinguish all the flaming arrows that the evil one and his army shoot at you. Put My helmet of salvation on your head, and put the sword of My Spirit—My Word—in your hands. Above all else, daughter, come to Me continually, in every circumstance you confront, with your requests for My assistance. Our continual fellowship will make you victorious in every demonic confrontation with the enemy.

EPHESIANS 6:12–18; PSALM 144:1–2, CEV

Prayer Declaration

I am dead to my sinful nature because God has made me alive with Christ. Because of His Son's sacrifice, God has forgiven all my sins, nailing them to the cross of Calvary. He has disarmed all demonic powers and authorities and allowed me to triumph over them through the work of His Son on the cross.

I WILL CAUSE YOU TO BREAK THROUGH ANY DEMONIC OPPOSITION

THROUGH YOUR PRAYERS to Me My power can flow. Never forget that My Word and My Holy Spirit are your source of power. Stand strong in Me and in the power of My might. I am a mighty man of war, and I will fight your battles for you. You can depend on My power and direction. I will be the strength of your life. Meditate upon My Word. Speak forth My Word with your mouth. I am the source for all your victories and breakthroughs. My Word contains wisdom and strategies for your warfare. As you study My Word, I will lead you forward to liberty and victory over every demonic force that comes against you. As you call upon Me, I will answer you and will show you great and mighty things that you do not know.

PSALM 144:1; EPHESIANS 6:10; JEREMIAH 33:3

Prayer Declaration

I praise my Lord who is my rock. He trains my hands for war and my fingers for battle. He is my loving God and my fortress, my stronghold and my deliverer, my shield in whom I take refuge.

YOU CAN COUNT ON MY READINESS TO HELP YOU

My DAUGHTER, I am ready to help you, so there is no weapon that is formed against you that will be successful. I have established you in My righteousness, and all forms of demonic oppression are far away from you. Don't be afraid of Satan's show of force, because I am with you. I have not given you a spirit of fear. I have given to you all my power through My Holy Spirit. I have filled you with My love, and I have given to you a sound mind. Stand secure in Me. Don't be afraid of Satan's intimidation. Don't worry about whether you have enough strength for the battles you must fight. You are My beloved daughter, and I have blessed you with every spiritual blessing from My place in heaven. I have delivered you from the power of darkness and have translated you into My kingdom where I dwell with My dear Son.

ISAIAH 54:17; 1 JOHN 4:4; COLOSSIANS 1:13,
THE MESSAGE

Prayer Declaration

Lord, You are my fortress. I live under Your protection, and I rest in Your powerful shadow. When I am in trouble, I will call out to You, and You will answer me with Your arm of protection. You will honor me and give me long life with Your saving power.

I Want to Show You What I Have for You

Stay in My presence, for I want to show You the blessings that I have for you. Because I love you so much, you have great favor with Me, and I give you favor with your fellow man as well. I will anoint your head with oil, and your life will overflow with My blessings. Goodness and mercy will surround your life as long as you live. You will reign in godly power in your life because of the great sacrifice of My Son, Jesus, for you. Each step you take will be bathed in My divine light, and the blood of My dear Son, Jesus, has cleansed you from all your sin. No evil will befall you, and no plague will come near your home and family. Stay hidden in My secret place, where you are rooted and grounded in My love.

Deuteronomy 28:13; Psalm 23:5–6;
Ephesians 3:16–17, cev

Prayer Declaration

Father, because You are my shepherd, I will never be in need. You will lead me along the right paths. If I walk through a valley as dark as death, I won't be afraid because You are with me. Your kindness and love will always be with me each day of my life.

LET ME REMIND YOU OF WHO YOU ARE

I HAVE SEEN the times when you felt alone…abandoned…helpless, and I want to remind you of who you really are. Allow My Holy Spirit to touch your spirit and confirm who you really are. I am Your Father; you are My daughter! There is an unbelievable inheritance waiting for you! My own dear Son gave His life so that you could live. You have been created anew and are clothed in My own righteousness. I have given you eternal life through My Son. I created you to do good works and gave you My promise that you can do all things through the power of My Son, who strengthens you. You have My mind; your life is hidden in Me; and because My Son lives in you, you have been filled with the hope of sharing in My glory. Through the work of My Son, all your needs will be supplied. You are Mine!

ROMANS 8:16–17; 2 CORINTHIANS 2:14, 17;
EPHESIANS 1:3–4

Prayer Declaration

*Father, You gave me Your Spirit to make me wise and
to help me understand what it means to know You.
Your light floods my heart with the hope of the glorious
blessings and the wonderful power You have for me.*

WHAT ARE YOU WILLING TO GIVE UP FOR ME?

MY DAUGHTER, DO you know that I take great delight in you? Your dedication to live your life by pleasing Me has caused Me to rejoice over you with singing. When I hear you renounce the things of this world that can only bring you destruction and death, My joy overflows. I have heard your prayers, and I take great delight in your obedience to My Word. Because you have given up all uncleanness, drunkenness, revelries, lewdness, fornication, and adultery, I have filled your life with My love. Instead of sinful hatred, contentions, jealousies, and outbursts of wrath, My joy flows through your life and My peace surrounds you. Allow the fruit of My Spirit to flow out of your life to others, because My love has made you more, so much more, than a conqueror on earth. Nothing will ever be able to separate you from Me because of My great love for you.

ZEPHANIAH 3:17; GALATIANS 5:16, 19–25;
ROMANS 8:37–39

Prayer Declaration

*I am victorious in everything, Father, because of Christ
who loves me. Nothing can separate us from God's love—
not life or death, not angels or spirits, not the present or
the future, and not powers above or powers below.*

REMEMBER THAT I AM ALL YOU NEED

MY DAUGHTER, YOU can always count on My unfailing love for you. I have filled the whole earth with My unfailing love. I will be a refuge for you, a strong tower against your foes. My endless supply of glorious riches will strengthen you with power through My Spirit in your inner being. Through your faith, My Son will dwell in your heart. I have dug the roots of My love deep within you, and I have established you in love. Grasp hold of My love, for it surpasses all knowledge and will fill you full of My presence. If you will trust in Me, I will fill you with joy and peace, and your life will overflow with hope by the power of My Holy Spirit. Faith will permeate in you, and My gifts of healing, miraculous powers, prophecy, discernment, and tongues and interpretation are yours for the taking.

PSALM 33:4–5; EPHESIANS 3:20;
1 CORINTHIANS 12:7–11

Prayer Declaration

I am redeemed from the curse of the law. I am redeemed from poverty. I am redeemed from sickness. I am redeemed from spiritual death. I overcome all because greater is He that is in me than he that is in the world.

BECAUSE OF WHO YOU ARE IN ME, YOUR FAMILY IS SAFE

My daughter, even though the heavens and earth may shake, I will be a shelter for My people. Be careful to obey My Word, so that it may go well with you and that you may increase greatly in a land flowing with milk and honey, just as I promised you. Fix My Word in your heart and mind, tie them as a symbol on your hands and bind them on your forehead. Teach them to your children when you sit at home, or walk along the road, or lie down to sleep. Establish My Word in your home so that your days and the days of your children may be many. I will be faithful to you through all your generations. My love will stand firm forever, and I will establish your family line forever. You will live to see your children's children walking in My ways.

Deuteronomy 6:1–3; 11:18–21; Psalms 89:1, 4;
4:7–8; 28:1–3

Prayer Declaration

*Because I respect You, Father, and obey Your laws, my field
will produce, and I will be happy and all will go well. My
husband and I will be fruitful, and just as an olive tree is rich
with olives, my home will be rich with healthy children.*

I Am in You, and You Are in Me

JUST AS MY Son is *in Me*, and I am *in Him*, so too I am *in you*. As long as My Word abides in you, you can ask Me for whatever you desire, and it will be yours. If you keep My Word, you will always abide in My love. I am telling you these things so that My joy may remain in you and that your joy may be full. You did not choose Me, but I chose you and appointed you that you should go and bear fruit. But remember always that My Son did not pray that I would take you out of this sinful world, but He prayed that I would keep you from the evil one in the world. I have sanctified you by My truth and sent you into the world so that the world can know Me and can love Me and My Son.

JOHN 14:20; JOHN 14:17, 25–27; 15:4–5, 7, CEV

Prayer Declaration

Holy Spirit, show me what is true. Keep living in me, for because You live, I will also live. You will help me and will teach me everything that is in Your Word. I have peace, the kind of peace only You can give. So I will not worry or be afraid.

January 15

MY BLESSINGS ARE FOR YOU

TODAY I AM giving you My promise of blessing, just as I blessed My people long ago. I will bless you and keep you. I will make My face to shine upon you and be gracious to you. I will lift up my countenance upon you and give you peace. Because you are my faithful daughter and obey My voice, I will make the work of your hands successful. I will help you to defeat your enemies and make your storehouses full. I will send rain on your land at just the right time, and you will have plenty of money to lend and will not need to borrow any for yourself. As long as you obey My Word, you will be wealthy and powerful, not poor and weak.

NUMBERS 6:22–27; DEUTERONOMY 28:1–14;
PSALMS 37:26; 68:19

Prayer Declaration

Father, let Your showers of blessing be upon my life. I am chosen by God, my sins are forgiven, and I am blessed. Daily You load me with benefits, and my seed is blessed. You will bless my latter end more than my beginning.

MY BLESSINGS ARE FOR YOUR FAMILY
AND LOVED ONES

YOUR FAMILY AND loved ones are a heritage and a reward
from Me. My blessings will be upon your family, and My
shield of protection will surround them. Have confidence in
Me, and I will make a place of refuge for your family. While
you walk in integrity, your children will be blessed after you.
Teach My ways to your children, so that I can continue to
pour My blessings upon them. My part is to bless your children, and your part is to teach them My ways. Talk about
them all the time—whether you are at home or away, in the
morning or at night. Teach your children to love My Word.
Tell your children of My great love for them. Remind them
of My Son's special love for children, and bring your children
into My presence.

PSALM 127:3; PROVERBS 14:26–27; MARK 10:13–16

Prayer Declaration

*I praise the Lord, for His angels are ever near to protect my
family. The Lord will perform His Word in my children.
Nothing will harm them. God Almighty will save my children, and they will delight in Him. All my loved ones will
be taught by the Lord, and great will be their peace.*

MY BLESSINGS ARE FOR YOUR LAND

IF YOU WILL trust in Me and live right, the land will be yours, and you will be safe. There has never been a time when I left My daughters helpless, and their children have never gone begging for food. If you continue to do right, you will live and be secure. I am on your side! If you remember My teachings, you will never take a wrong step. I will defend you and will give you and your loved ones a bright future. I will always protect you. You can come to Me in times of trouble. Because you are My child, and I am Your Father, I will make the nations of this world your inheritance, and the ends of the earth will be your possession. Test Me, and you will see that I throw open the floodgates of heaven and pour out so many blessings for you that you will not have room enough for them.

PSALMS 2:8; 27:9–11; MALACHI 3:10–18

Prayer Declaration

*Lord, I have placed my trust in You! Because I obey
Your Word, I am always in Your care, and what You
have given to me will belong to my family forever.*

MY FAVOR WILL POUR OUT UPON YOU

MY DAUGHTER, REMEMBER that I am strong and mighty. I will scatter your enemies with My strong arm, and I have extended My right hand of faithfulness to you. My love and faithfulness will go before Me and bless you because you have honored Me as your God. I will lead you to walk in the light of My presence all day long. My favor will be your strength. Commit whatever you do to Me, and I will establish your plans. I will cause everything to work out to its proper end. I will take pleasure in your honesty, and you will see the brightness of My face, for My favor will be on you like a rain cloud in spring. When You call upon Me, I will arise and will have compassion on you, and I will show My favor to you.

PSALM 89:1–29; PROVERBS 16:12–16

Prayer Declaration

Father, I am calling to You. Look upon me with Your great love and favor. I will praise Your name in song and glorify You with thanksgiving. I will seek You, and I will place my hope in You.

I Will Reveal Each Step You Are to Take

Come to Me, and I will teach you My ways so that you can walk in My paths. If you will walk in obedience to me and keep My requirements, then you will govern My house and have charge of My courts, and I will give you a place among these standing here. Because you delight in Me, I will make your steps firm. Though you stumble, you will not fall, for I will uphold you with My hand. Your steps have held to My paths, and you have kept yourself from the ways of violent men. Therefore I will show you the wonders of My great love and will save you by My right hand. I will keep you as the apple of My eye and will hide you in the shadow of My wings.

Isaiah 2:3; Jeremiah 7:23; Mark 4:11; Psalm 17:6–8

Prayer Declaration

Lord, I am blessed because I walk according to Your Word. You have laid down precepts for me to obey, and my ways will be steadfast in obeying Your ways. I will praise You with an upright heart as I obey Your decrees, and You will never forsake me.

I WILL SHARE MY SECRET PLANS WITH YOU

I AM A God who reveals secrets, and I will reveal My secrets unto you. I will help you to understand things that I have kept secret from the foundation of the world. You will understand My revelation of My will and purpose for your life. I will open your eyes to behold wondrous things out of My Word. The secret things belong to Me, but those things that I will reveal to You will belong to you and your children forever, that you may follow all My Word. When your soul is weary with sorrow, My Word will strengthen and comfort you. My Word is eternal, and it stands firm in the heavens. My faithfulness to you will continue through all your generations. Let My Word be a lamp to your feet and a light upon your path.

MATTHEW 13:35; PSALM 119

Prayer Declaration

Father, I will praise You with an upright heart as I learn Your righteous laws. I have hidden Your Word in my heart that I might not sin against You. Keep me from deceitful ways; be gracious to me and teach me Your law.

JANUARY 21

I Will Shine My Light Upon Your Path

I WILL LIGHT your candle and enlighten your darkness. My light will shine upon your head. I will give you the treasures of darkness and the hidden riches in My secret places. I will let you understand the deep things in My heart. You will be able to understand the parables I have spoken and the mystery of My will for you. I will unveil the mysteries of My kingdom, and I will speak to you with revelation. If you will turn your ear to wisdom and apply your heart to understanding, and call out for insight and understanding, then you will understand My knowledge, for I will give wisdom, knowledge, and understanding. Trust in Me with all your heart, and lean not on your own understanding; in all your ways acknowledge Me, and I will make your paths straight.

PSALM 119:111–112; 1 CORINTHIANS 2:10;
PROVERBS 3:5–6

Prayer Declaration

Father, I kneel before you today and pray that out of Your glorious riches you will strengthen me with power through Your Holy Spirit who resides within me. Dwell in my heart in Your fullness. I am rooted and established in Your love. I know Your love surpasses any other knowledge, and I want to be filled to the measure of your fullness.

22   WOMEN'S DAILY DECLARATIONS FOR SPIRITUAL WARFARE

I Will Position You in Heavenly Places

I AM THE Creator of all things and have given you blessings that cannot be measured. I have caused you to understand the mysterious plan that has always been hidden in My mind so that You can be filled with My power and authority. For you are not preparing for warfare against flesh and blood, but you will face warfare against the rulers of the darkness of this age, and against the spiritual hosts of wickedness in the heavenly places. My power in you will release My angels to war against the spirits in the heavens who would block your prayers from being answered. I will give you an open heaven and will bind any demonic interference from the heavens through My name.

EPHESIANS 1

Prayer Declaration

*I am sitting in heavenly places in Christ, far above all
principalities, powers, might, and dominion. God has
positioned me in the heavens and allowed me to bind the
principalities and powers that operate against my life through
His power. I bind the prince of the power of the air, and I
pray for the floodgates of heaven to be opened over my life.*

THE POWERS OF THE HEAVENS WILL NOT HINDER YOU

MY DAUGHTER, JUST as I opened the heavens for Ezekiel and allowed him to see visions of Me, so I will open the heavens over your life and let you see My visions. The prince of the power of the air will be bound, and My angels will war against any spirit in the heavens who has been assigned to keep your prayers from rising up to Me. My voice will thunder down hailstones and coals of fire against your enemies. I will drop the dew of My heaven over you, and I will come down to meet with you. The rain of My Holy Spirit will fall upon you, and the heavens will be filled with praise for My mighty wonders. You will be filled with the knowledge of My ways and will make known My manifold wisdom to the principalities and powers in the heavenly places.

HAGGAI 2:6–7; PSALM 89:5; EPHESIANS 3:10

Prayer Declaration

I receive the rain and blessing from heaven upon my life in the name of Jesus. I bind the prince of the power of the air and pray for the floodgates of heaven to be opened over my life. I will see visions, and my house will be filled with the glory of God. The Lord will release His manifold wisdom to me, and I will make known His knowledge to the heavens and earth.

I Will Awaken You With My Presence Each Morning

I HAVE COMMANDED the morning and caused the dawn to know its place, that it might take hold of the ends of the earth and shake the wicked out of it. Because you are upright, daughter, I will give you dominion over the foolish of this world. My glorious power will be seen, for you will wear the sacred robe of My righteousness and will shine like the morning sun with My strength. My light will break forth like the morning, and My healing will spring forth speedily. I will hear your voice in the morning as you lay your requests before Me and wait in expectation. I am a fortress for you, and a refuge in your times of trouble. I will satisfy you in the morning with My unfailing love, and you will be able to sing for joy and be glad all your days.

JOB 38:12; PSALMS 110:3; 143:1, 8

Prayer Declaration

My soul waits for you, Lord, more than watchmen wait for the morning. I have put my hope in You because of Your unfailing love for me. Your love is like the morning mist, like the early dew. Lord, Your going forth is prepared as the morning, and I pray that You will come as the rain, the latter and former rain upon the earth.

The Evils of the Day Will Never Enslave You

My daughter, I will visit you every morning and will show forth My salvation in your life from day to day. My judgments will come upon your enemies morning by morning. Because of My great mercy toward you, your enemies will not enslave you. My compassions will not fail you; they are new every morning. My faithfulness will never cease, and I will be your portion forever. Therefore place your hope in Me. I will be with you, and I am mighty to save. I take great delight in you, and I will quiet you with My love. I will rejoice over you with singing. I will remove sorrow from you, and I will deal with all who oppress you. I will rescue the lame and gather those who have been scattered. I will give you honor and praise and will restore your fortunes before your very eyes.

Psalm 91:3–5; Lamentations 3:22–23;
Zephaniah 3:17–20

Prayer Declaration

Jesus, just as You stood on the shore early in the morning and called out to Your disciples, You will make Your presence known to me in the morning hours and will call out for me to come into Your presence. Direct my steps to my miracle, Lord, just as You guided the disciples to a miracle catch of fish that morning. Feed me, as You fed them.

I Will Give You Sweet Rest in the Night

Do not be filled with fears in the night hours, My daughter, for I have promised to be your fortress, your place of safety. I have spread My wings over you, and I will keep you secure. You don't need to worry about dangers at night for you will not be harmed even though thousands may fall all around you. Remember how I sent My angels to guard My servant Paul when he was bound by chains in a prison cell. My angels filled his prison cell with light and caused his chains to fall off. They escorted him out of his cell, through the prison gates, and opened the city gates to let him escape. You too can count on My angels' protection in the night hours. Fear not, and listen for the sound of My voice, for I will fill your heart with My song in the night hours.

Psalm 91:1–7; Acts 12:6–10; Psalm 42:8

Prayer Declaration

You are my shield, and You give me victory and great honor. I pray to You, and You answer from Your sacred hill. I sleep and wake up refreshed because You, Lord, protect me. I will rest at night because You give me sleep. I take authority over every demon that is released against my family and me at night. I will meditate upon my Lord in the night watches.

YOU WILL SEE VISIONS AND DREAM DREAMS FROM ME

MY DAUGHTER, I reveal Myself to my servants in visions, and I speak to them in dreams. Just as I gave my knowledge and understanding to Daniel and his friends, I will fill you with My knowledge and understanding. Just as Daniel could understand visions and dreams of all kinds, so too, if you serve Me with all your heart, will I give you understanding of visions and dreams from Me. When I give you My visions and dreams, pay close attention to all I say, for you too have been brought to this moment for a very special purpose.

ACTS 2:17–18; DANIEL 1:17; EZEKIEL 40:1–4

Prayer Declaration

Lord, I do not fear the darkness of night, for I wait expectantly for Your visions and dreams to fill me with understanding and knowledge for Your people. You awaken me morning by morning, and you waken my ear to hear as the learned hear. You show forth Your salvation in my life from day to day. Let Your angels guard and protect me at night, and I will show forth Your glory every day.

MY KINGDOM WILL BE ESTABLISHED IN YOUR LIFE

MY KINGDOM COME, My will be done, on earth as it is in heaven. My kingdom will advance and be established through the preaching and teaching of My Word, and through My miracles of healing. Let the gates of your life and city be opened for the King of glory to come in. I am robed in majesty and armed with strength; indeed, the whole world is established, firm, and secure because My throne was established long ago—from all eternity. Do not be afraid, little one, for it has pleased Me to give you the kingdom. Let men know of My mighty acts and the glorious majesty of My kingdom. Let the kingdoms of this world become the kingdoms of My Son, Jesus Christ.

MATTHEW 4:23; PSALMS 24:7; 103:19–22; 145:12

Prayer Declaration

Your kingdom come, Lord, Your will be done. Lord, You reign. You are clothed with majesty and strength. Your throne is established of old. You are from everlasting. I receive the kingdom because it is Your good pleasure to give it to me. Let me speak of the glory of Your kingdom and talk of Your power.

MY INCREASE WILL BE YOURS

I WILL REMEMBER you and will bless you. I will bless your house and all those who fear Me, small and great alike. Because of My great love and faithfulness to you, I will increase you more and more, both you and your children. The silver and gold idols of this world have been made by human hands. They have mouths but cannot speak; eyes, but they cannot see; ears, but they cannot hear. Those who make them will be like them, and so will all who trust in them. But you, My daughter, trust only in Me. I am your help and shield. You who once walked in darkness have seen a great light. I have enlarged your life and increased your joy. I have shattered the yoke that burdened you, the bar across your shoulder, and the rod of those who tried to oppress you.

1 CHRONICLES 4:10; PSALM 115:1–14; ISAIAH 9:1–5

Prayer Declaration

Lord, not to us but to Your name be the glory, because of Your love and faithfulness. You will remember us and will bless us. You will bless all those who fear Your name and will cause me to flourish, both me and my children. I will extol Your great name both now and forevermore.

I Will Enlarge Each Part of Your Life

I will break off of your life any limitations and restrictions placed on your life by any evil spirit. I will enlarge each part of your life and will keep you from evil. My kingdom and government will increase in your life, and you will receive deliverance and enlargement for your life. I will let you increase exceedingly. You will increase in wisdom and stature and in strength. You will confound your adversaries as My grace and favor increase in your life. My Word will increase in your life, and the years of your life will be increased. You will flourish like a palm tree and grow like a cedar in Lebanon. They will take root in your house and will do well. They will be trees that stay healthy and fruitful to all your generations.

Isaiah 9:7; 60:4–5; Acts 9:22; Psalm 92:12

Prayer Declaration

Cast out my enemies, and enlarge my borders. Enlarge my heart so I can run the way of Your commandments. Enlarge my steps so I can receive Your wealth and prosperity. Let me increase in the knowledge of God, and let me increase and abound in love.

YOU ARE A JOINT HEIR WITH MY SON, JESUS CHRIST

I AM THE One who breaks open the way, and I will go up before you; you will break through the gates that try to hold you, and you will go out. You will be a fruitful vine, planted near a spring, and your branches will climb over any wall that attempts to hold you in. My eyes will be open to your supplication, and I will listen whenever you call to Me. Rejoice, for I will not cast off My people, nor will I forsake My inheritance. If you fear that your foot will slip, My mercy will hold you up. When you are filled with anxieties within, My comfort will delight your soul. I will be your defense and the rock of your refuge. I have sealed you with My Holy Spirit of promise, who is the guarantee of your inheritance.

PSALMS 2:7–8; 94:18–19; EPHESIANS 1:13–14

Prayer Declaration

I am a joint heir with Jesus Christ. Give me the heathen for my inheritance and the uttermost part of the earth for my possession. Let my line go through all the earth, and my words to the end of the world. Let me grow in grace and in the knowledge of Jesus Christ. I will flourish like a palm tree and grow like a cedar in Lebanon.

FEBRUARY

Recognizing the Enemy's Weapons

I Am the God Who Answers by Fire

When My servant Elijah stood before the four hundred false prophets of the enemy and called upon My name, I answered his prayer with My all-consuming fire. When the people saw My fire, they fell to the ground and worshipped Me. In My power and strength, Elijah destroyed the enemy's false prophets. Remember this, My daughter, and call upon My name when you are overpowered by the enemy. I will come down with My righteous fire and destroy all your enemies. I am the Lord who reigns over all the earth. My holy fire goes before Me and consumes all your foes on every side. The lightning of my power lights up the world. The earth sees and trembles, and the mountains melt like wax before Me.

1 Kings 18; Psalm 97:1–5

Prayer Declaration

Father, You are the God who answers by fire. Release Your fire and burn up the works of darkness. Let Your fire burn in my eyes, my heart, my belly, my mouth, and my feet. Let Your fire be in my tongue to preach and prophesy. Make me a minister of Your fire.

I Will Purify Your Life With My Fire

ON THE DAY that I come, I will come like a furnace that purifies silver, and I will purify you as I purify gold and silver. I will redeem you from every lawless deed and purify you for Myself to be My own special people, zealous for good works. Draw near to Me, and I will draw near to you. Humble yourself in My sight, and when My purifying work is complete, I will lift you up and purge you with My holy fire so that you become an offering before Me of righteousness. I have tested you and refined you as silver is refined. I have allowed you to pass through fire and through water, but I brought you out to rich fulfillment. I have preserved your soul among the living, and I will not allow your feet to be moved.

MALACHI 3:2–3; ZECHARIAH 13:9; PSALM 66:8–12

Prayer Declaration

Lord, purify my life with Your fire. Refine me like silver. Purge my life from sin and imperfection as You purge gold and silver that I may become an offering before You of righteousness. I will live my life by denying ungodliness and world lusts, and I will live soberly, righteously, and godly in this present age.

MY FIRE WILL CONSUME THE WORKS OF WITCHCRAFT AND OCCULTISM

Do NOT TURN away from Me to serve other gods, My daughter, for if you turn your children away from Me to serve other gods, My anger will burn against you and will quickly destroy you. Break down the altars of witchcraft and burn any occultic idols in the fire. For you are a people holy to Me. I have chosen you out of all the peoples on the face of the earth to be My people, My treasured possession. Do not test My promises to you and turn to witchcraft and idols, for I will cause a fire to consume your wickedness just as I did with the children of Israel.

ACTS 19:18–20; DEUTERONOMY 7:3–6;
PSALM 106:16–23

Prayer Declaration

*Lord, release Your fire and burn up the idols of this land.
Let the works of witchcraft and occultism be burned in
Your fire. Let Your flame be kindled against wicked spirits,
and let demons be exposed and cast out with Your fire.*

I WILL DESTROY THE WORKS OF LUST AND PERVERSION

MY DAUGHTER, DO not be fooled. Anyone who keeps on sinning belongs to the devil. He has sinned from the beginning, but My Son came to destroy all that he has done. If anyone loves the world, My love is not in him. For all that is in the world—the lust of the flesh, the lust of the eyes, and the pride of life—is not of Me, but is of the world. The world is passing away, and the lust of it. When you ask why the land perishes and burns up like a wilderness so that no one can pass through, I will respond: Because you have forsaken My law which I set before you, and have not obeyed My voice, nor walked according to it. Therefore I will scatter those who do the works of lust and perversion and will send a sword after them until I have consumed them.

GENESIS 19:12–13; 1 JOHN 2:16; JEREMIAH 9:12–16

Prayer Declaration

Let the spirits of lust and perversion be destroyed with Your fire. Pass through the land and burn up all wickedness and perversion from out of it. The world is passing away, and the lust of it, but he who does the will of God abides forever.

I WILL REBUKE YOUR ENEMIES WITH FLAMES OF FIRE

LET YOUR HEART rejoice, for I have promised that My faithful daughters will flourish like grass, and I will extend My hand to bestow blessings on them. But I will show My fury to My enemies and to those who oppress My daughters. Do not fear that you will be overcome by your enemies, for I will rebuke your enemies with flames of fire. Stand boldly before your enemies and tell them: "This is what the Sovereign LORD says: I am about to set fire to you, and it will consume all your trees, both green and dry. The blazing flame will not be quenched, and every face from south to north will be scorched by it. Everyone will see that I the LORD have kindled it; it will not be quenched."

ISAIAH 66:14–16; EZEKIEL 20:47–48, NIV

Prayer Declaration

*Let Your flame come and burn up all my enemies,
Lord—all those who seek to bring oppression and captivity to Your followers. Let Your holy fire burn them until
none of their wickedness remains. Let them not be able
to deliver themselves from the power of Your flames.*

MY SWORD WILL COME AGAINST
THE POWERS OF HELL

LET MY FAITHFUL daughters rejoice in My protection, for I take great delight in them, and I crown their faithfulness with victory. I will honor your praises as they rise to Me. I have placed My two-edged sword in your hands so that you can inflict My vengeance on the nations and punishment on the peoples, to bind their kings with fetters, their nobles with shackles of iron, to carry out the sentence written against them. See now that there is no god besides me. I put to death and I bring to life. I have wounded and I will heal, and no one can deliver out of My hand. As surely as I live forever, when I sharpen My flashing sword and My hand grasps it in judgment, I will take vengeance on My adversaries and repay those who hate Me.

PSALMS 45:3–4; 149:6–9; ISAIAH 27:1

Prayer Declaration

I release the sword of the Lord against the powers of hell in the name of Jesus. Send Your angels with flaming swords to fight my battles in the heavens. Let Your enemies fall by the sword. Take vengeance on my adversaries and rise up to stand victoriously over all of Satan's demon warriors.

MY ARROWS OF LIGHT WILL DESTROY THE KINGDOM OF DARKNESS

I HAVE PROMISED that I will send out My arrows and scatter the enemy. Do not fear the kingdom of darkness, for I will protect you. Through My unfailing love you will not be shaken. When the enemy appears before you for battle, I will burn them up as in a blazing furnace. My fire will consume them. Though they plot evil against you and devise wicked schemes, they cannot succeed. My arrows will flash like lightning, and I will destroy them. My sharp arrows will pierce their hearts. I am a righteous judge. I will display My wrath against the kingdom of darkness every day. I will sharpen My sword and will bend and string my bow. I have prepared My deadly weapons and have made ready my flaming arrows.

PSALMS 18:13–15; 21:9–12; 7:11–13

Prayer Declaration

*I release the arrow of the Lord's deliverance in my life.
Ordain and release Your arrows against my persecutors.
Send Your arrows, and scatter the enemy. Let your
arrow go forth as lightning against the enemy. Break their
bones, and pierce them through with Your arrows.*

I WILL BREAK ALL GENERATIONAL CURSES IN YOUR LIFE

MY DAUGHTER, I will bless you and make your name great, and you will be a blessing. I will bless those who bless you, and whoever curses you I will curse. I have redeemed you from the curse of the law. I will break all oaths, vows, and pacts made with the devil by your ancestors. I will break all curses spoken by agents of Satan against your life or the lives of your generations. I have given you the authority through My Son, Jesus, to command inherited curses to leave. My power and authority have broken any legal rights the generational spirits of wickedness have had to operate in your life. Through My Son, Jesus, you have My authority to command all hereditary spirits of lust, rejection, fear, sickness, infirmity, disease, anger, hatred, confusion, failure, and poverty to leave your life.

2 CHRONICLES 34:24; MATTHEW 4:23; 9:35; 10:1

Prayer Declaration

I am redeemed from the curse of the law. I break all generational curses of pride, lust, perversion, rebellion, witchcraft, idolatry, poverty, rejection, fear, confusion, addiction, death, and destruction in the name of Jesus. I break all spoken curses and negative words that have been spoken over my life.

I WILL BREAK THE CURSE OF SICKNESS AND DISEASE

IF YOU DO not obey Me and do not carefully follow My words, I will plague you with disease, fever, and inflammation until you are destroyed. But if you will serve Me, the Lord your God, My blessing will be on your food and water. I have redeemed your life from the pit, and I have crowned you with love and compassion. I satisfy all your desires with good things, so that your youth is renewed like the eagle's. My precious Son has destroyed the curse of the Law and has redeemed you and healed you by His sacrifice. He took your pain and bore your suffering. By His wounds you are healed. And He has given My daughters the authority to drive out demons and to cure diseases. Therefore go forth and proclaim My kingdom on earth and heal the sick.

DEUTERONOMY 7:15; PSALM 103:1–5; LUKE 9:1–2

Prayer Declaration

Father, I am Your child, and You are my God. I stand in Your righteousness and in the wholeness and life that You have given to me through the sacrifice of Your Son, Jesus. Your Son, Jesus, took all my sins and sicknesses upon Himself, and He has given me and my loved ones the privilege of walking in wholeness—body, soul, and spirit.

I BIND THE GENERATIONAL REBELLION AGAINST MY HOLY SPIRIT

MY DAUGHTER, DO not disobey Me and hide rebellion against Me in your heart as the children of Israel and King Saul did. In My love and mercy I redeemed them, and I lifted them up and carried them. Do not grieve My Holy Spirit, but keep as your pattern sound teaching, faith, and love in Christ Jesus. Guard the good deposit that was entrusted to you—guard it with the help of the Holy Spirit who lives in you. I will come to you and will bind the generational rebellion against My Holy Spirit that began with My children of Israel. I am the God of hope, and I will fill you with all joy and peace as you trust in Me, so that you may overflow with hope by the power of My Spirit.

ISAIAH 63:10; ACTS 7:51; 2 TIMOTHY 1:13;
ROMANS 15:13

Prayer Declaration

I praise You, Father, for You have loosened my spirit from the spirit of rebellion against Your Spirit that began with Your children in the wilderness. I will guard the good deposit of new life that you have given me with the help of Your Holy Spirit who now lives in me.

I BREAK THE CURSE OF DEATH SPOKEN AGAINST AMERICA

JUST AS I gave the Promised Land to My children of Israel, so I gave America to your descendants because of their faithfulness and desire to worship Me. But just as I placed a curse on the land of Israel when My children disobeyed Me and failed to live according to My covenant with them, so a curse of death will rest on your land for your disobedience to Me. If you will turn back to Me, humble yourselves, and turn from your wicked ways, then I will forgive your sins and heal your land. Those who place their hope in Me will inherit the land and will live in peace. You are My sheep, and I am your God, and I will take care of you.

2 CHRONICLES 7:14; PSALM 37:3, 9; EZEKIEL 34:25–31

Prayer Declaration

Father, we humble ourselves and pray that You will forgive our wicked ways. Forgive our sins and heal our land. Our God, You save us, and Your fearsome deeds answer our prayers for justice!

UNGODLY COVENANTS MADE BY YOUR ANCESTORS ARE BROKEN

IF YOU VIOLATE My covenant and go and serve other gods and bow down to them, My anger will burn against you, and you will quickly perish from the good land I have given you. But if you do not follow other gods to your own harm, then I will let you live in this place, in the land I gave your fore-fathers forever and ever. I have laid a sure foundation, and if you rely on My precious cornerstone and make My justice your measuring line and righteousness your plumb line, then I will disannul all ungodly covenants your ancestors made with idols, demons, false religious, or ungodly organizations in the name of My Son, Jesus. I will take hold of your hand, My daughter, and will keep you and make you to be a covenant for the people and a light for unbelievers.

EXODUS 23:31–33; MATTHEW 5:33; ISAIAH 42:6

Prayer Declaration

I break and disannul all ungodly covenants, oaths, and pledges I have made with my lips in the name of Jesus. I break and disannul all covenants with death and hell made by my ancestors in the name of Jesus. I command all demons that claim any legal right to my life through covenants to come out in the name of Jesus.

THE BLOOD OF MY SON HAS PLACED YOU IN COVENANT RELATIONSHIP WITH ME

THROUGH THE PRECIOUS blood of My Son, Jesus, you have entered into a new covenant relationship with Me. His blood has given you the confidence to enter directly into My presence. Come and draw near to Me with a sincere heart and with the full assurance that faith in My Son has given to you. His blood has cleansed you from a guilty conscience and has washed you with pure water. Hold unswervingly to the hope in Christ that you have professed, for I am faithful. Spur one another to live your lives in holiness and love. I am light, and in Me there is no darkness at all. Therefore walk in My light; have fellowship with those who also walk in My light and who have been purified by the blood of My Son.

HEBREWS 9:24–28; 10:19–24; 1 JOHN 1:9–10

Prayer Declaration

I stand before You washed in the blood of Your Son and robed in His righteousness. You have raised me from death to life and have broken all the chains of wickedness that had bound me in sin. I have been set free from sin and have willingly become a slave to Your righteousness.

I Have Established a Covenant of Love With You

THOUGH THE MOUNTAINS be shaken and the hills be removed, yet My unfailing love for you will not be shaken nor My covenant of peace be removed. I chose you, My daughter, and set My affection on you because I love you. Know therefore that I am the Lord your God. I am a faithful God, and I will keep My covenant of love to a thousand generations of those who love Me and keep My commandments. I will love you and bless you and increase your numbers. I will bless the fruit of your womb, the crops of your land, the calves of your herds, and the lambs of your flocks in the land I have given you. You will be blessed more than any other people, and I will keep you free from every disease. No one will be able to stand up against you; you will destroy them.

DEUTERONOMY 7:12–24

Prayer Declaration

I am convinced that neither death nor life, neither angels nor demons, neither the present nor the future, nor any powers, neither height nor depth, nor anything else in all creation, will be able to separate us from the love of God that is in Christ Jesus our Lord.

Prepare to Engage the Enemy

My daughter, prepare for battle! As a good soldier of My Son, Christ Jesus, you must endure your share of suffering. Your enemies are My enemies, and just as I hate those who rebel and refuse to obey Me, so you must also hate My enemies. Separate yourself from Satan and from anyone who gets entangled with the affairs of this life. Remember the power available to you through My Son. There is power in the blood of My Son. His blood cleanses you from all sin. Give no place to the devil, but be sure that you operate in righteousness. My righteousness will give you confidence and boldness. My righteous daughters are as bold as lions. Engage the enemy boldly, and My protection will be your covering.

Proverbs 28:1; 18:37; 2 Timothy 2:3, 14

Prayer Declaration

Father, You have seated me through Christ in heavenly places, far above all principalities and powers. You have equipped me to engage the enemy and have promised that I will be victorious through You. I stand boldly ready to use Your weapons of warfare to utterly destroy the enemy and all the works of darkness. I will not turn back until they are all destroyed.

UNDERSTAND MY POWER AND AUTHORITY

I USE ORDINARY people to accomplish My purposes. Your ability to overcome in spiritual warfare comes from My power and authority. Do not base your faith on how you feel; base your faith on My Word. I have given you the legal right to use the name of My Son, Jesus. His name is above every other name. Authority in His name is recognized by the enemy. You will be able to cast out demons in His name. You can bind the works of darkness in His name. Through His name, and in the power you will receive from My Holy Spirit, you will be able to do exceedingly abundantly according to the power that operates through you. Fear not; prepare to engage the enemy.

EPHESIANS 6:10–12; LUKE 10:19; ACTS 1:8

Prayer Declaration

Father, through Your power and authority I will confront the powers of darkness. In Your Son's name I will defeat Satan and all his demonic warriors. You have given me the ability to endure and withstand hardship, adversity, and stress. I will be persistent in dealing with the enemy, and because of who I am in You I will be victorious.

I WILL CAUSE YOU TO DWELL IN SAFETY

I HAVE SENT My angels to surround you and to cause you to dwell in safety. They will deliver you from all danger and will surround you with My protection. I will hold you up, and you will be safe. My eyes are turned on My righteous daughters, and My ears are attentive to their cries. I will deliver you from all your troubles. The name of My Son is a fortified tower for you, and you can run to it where you will be safe. Do not be afraid, for I will guide you safely wherever you go. You can lie down and sleep, for I have made you to dwell in safety. I am Your God, and I will keep you safe and will protect you forever from the wicked who freely strut around in wickedness.

PSALMS 34:7–22; 78:52; 12:5

Prayer Declaration

You will answer me, Lord, when I call to You, and will give me relief from my distress. You will have mercy on me and hear my prayer. You will grant peace in my family, in my land, and no one will cause me to be afraid. You will walk with me and will be My God, and I will be Your faithful servant.

HUMILITY AND SUBMISSION TO ME WILL PROTECT YOU

I HAVE HEARD the desire of the humble, and I will prepare your heart and cause My ear to hear. I am great and mighty in power, and I will lift up the humble. But I will cast the wicked down to the ground. The highway of the upright avoids evil, and those who guard their ways preserve their lives. Pride goes before destruction and a haughty spirit before a fall. But how much better it is to be lowly in spirit, for I will instruct the humble in the way they should go. I will prosper them and bless the one who trusts only in Me. You who are younger, submit yourselves to your elders, and clothe yourselves with humility toward one another. For I will oppose the proud, but I will show favor to the humble. Humble yourself under My mighty hand, and I will lift you up in due time.

ISAIAH 57:15; PSALMS 10:17–18; 147:5–6;
1 PETER 5:5–6

Prayer Declaration

Father, in humility and submission I stand before You. I have prepared my heart to do Your will and have strengthened my spirit to follow after Your ways. Cover me with Your protection, for I have submitted myself to You, to Your Word, and to Your Holy Spirit.

RECOGNIZING THE ENEMY'S WEAPONS

YOU ARE THE APPLE OF MY EYE

I HAVE PROBED your heart and tested you, and I know that you have no evil plans and your mouth has not transgressed against Me. You have kept yourself from the ways of the violent by following My commandments. Your steps have held to My paths, and your feet have not stumbled. When you call to Me, I will answer you. I will turn my ear to you and hear your prayer. I will show you the wonders of My great love and will save you by My right hand. Because you are the apple of My eye, I will confront your enemies and bring them down. My mighty sword will rescue you from the wicked. I will vindicate you, and you will see My face when you awake and will be satisfied with seeing My likeness and protection.

PSALM 17

Prayer Declaration

Lord, You found me in a desert land, a howling wilderness, and You encircled me and instructed me and kept me as the apple of Your eye. You have promised to shake Your hand against those who dare to touch the apple of Your eye with trouble. You will cause my enemies to become spoil for Your servants, and by this will everyone know that I am Your inheritance and You have chosen to dwell in my midst.

I WILL BE YOUR DEFENSE AND REFUGE

I HAVE GIVEN you refuge in the shadow of My wings, and I
will keep you in safety until the disaster has passed. My glory
will be a canopy of protection for you. It will be a shelter and
shade from the heat of the day, and a refuge and hiding place
from the storm and rain. I am your shelter from the wind and
your refuge in the storm. I will be like streams of water in
the desert and the shadow of a great rock in a thirsty land. I
have put My words in your mouth and covered you with the
shadow of My hand. Gladness and joy will overtake you, and
sorrow and sighing will flee away. I am He who comforts you.

PSALM 91; ISAIAH 4:6; 32:1–2; 51:11–16

Prayer Declaration

*I will trust in the covering of Your wings, and in the shadow
of Your wings I will trust. Be my defense and refuge in
times of trouble. I will sing of Your strength. In the morning I will sing of Your love, for You are my fortress. You are
my strength. I sing praise to You, for on You I can rely.*

I Will Be a Shield for You in Battle

I will contend with those who contend with you, My daughter, and will fight against those who fight against you. Take up my shield and armor, for I will arise and come to your aid. I will brandish my spear and javelin against those who pursue you. I am your salvation. Those who seek your life will be disgraced and put to shame. I will turn back those who plot your ruin. They will be like the chaff before the wind, for My mighty angel will drive them away. The path that your enemies take will be dark and slippery. Because they dug a pit for you, I will cause ruin to overtake them by surprise. The net they hid to entrap you will ensnare them instead, and they will fall into a pit of ruin.

Psalms 35:1–10; 119:114–117

Prayer Declaration

Lord, You are a shield to me and my hiding place from my enemies. You will surround me with Your shield of protection and will bring down my enemies. I will not be afraid of ten thousand that have set themselves against me, because You are a shield for me. You are a strong tower from all my enemies. Spread Your protection over me, and I will rejoice and praise Your name.

I WILL STRETCH OUT MY ARM TO DELIVER YOU

THERE IS NO other like Me among all the heavenly beings. I am mighty, and My faithfulness surrounds you. I will crush and scatter your enemies with My strong arm. I am the Lord, and I will bring you out from under the yoke of your oppressors. I will free you and will redeem you with my outstretched arm and with mighty acts of judgment. I will stretch out My right hand, and the earth will swallow your enemies. With My unfailing love I will lead you to My holy dwelling. Terror and dread will fall on your enemies, and by the power of My arm they will be as still as a stone until you have passed by in safety.

ISAIAH 52:10; PSALM 89:6–13; EXODUS 15:12–16

Prayer Declaration

*No one has an arm like You, Lord, full of power and might.
Your hand is strong, and Your right hand is held high.
You will stretch out Your arm and deliver me, and rid me
out of all bondage. Let fear and dread fall upon the enemy by the greatness of Your arm until I pass over. Favor
me, and let Your right arm bring me into my possession.*

THE POWER IN MY HANDS WILL BE RELEASED IN YOUR LIFE

I WILL RELEASE My power and might against the enemy by My right hand. I will show you the path of life. In My presence is fullness of joy, and at My right hand are pleasures forevermore. Do not be afraid, My daughter, but follow close behind Me, for My right hand upholds you. My glory covers the heavens and My praise has filled the earth. Like the sunrise, rays flash from My hands where My power is hidden. I have shown My people the power of My works. The works of My hands are faithful and just, and all My precepts are trustworthy. They are established forever and ever and enacted in faithfulness and uprightness.

1 CHRONICLES 29:11–12; PSALMS 16:11; 111:6–8

Prayer Declaration

Lord, let the power in Your hands be released in my life.
Your mighty works are performed by Your hands. You laid
Your hands on the sick, and they recovered. You lifted up
Your hands and blessed Your people. With Your hands You
have given me the power and authority to defeat my enemies. I am delivered from the power of Satan unto You,
O Lord, and I am strong in Your power and might.

MY POWER AND MIGHT WILL
SCATTER THE ENEMY

MY POWER AND might will deliver you from your enemies. I will be a fortress for you against brutal people who attack you and want to kill you. Do not fear when they are ready to attack. I am the Lord God All-Powerful, and I will be your protection. Why are you so frightened when they plan their nighttime attacks with curses and confidence that no one can hear them? Have I not told you that My mighty power will make them tremble and fall? Don't you know? Haven't you heard? I am your eternal God, Creator of the earth, and I never get weary or tired. I give strength to those who are weary, so that you will be strong like an eagle soaring upward on wings.

PSALM 59:1–12; ISAIAH 40:10–11, 28–31

Prayer Declaration

Father, You have given to me the same great and mighty power that You used to defeat my enemies. Your power raised up Your Son from the dead, and I have access to that power to overcome all my enemies and live victoriously through You. Your glorious power will give me patience and strength to be victorious over Satan's evil intentions.

RECOGNIZING THE ENEMY'S WEAPONS

SIGNS, WONDERS, AND MIRACLES ARE RELEASED BY MY SPIRIT

IN THESE LAST days I will pour out My Spirit on all people. My Holy Spirit will give dreams and visions to your sons and daughters. All My daughters will prophesy. I will show you signs and wonders in the heavens above and on the earth. Many will call on My name and be saved. I have many different kinds of gifts for My daughters, but My Holy Spirit is the One who distributes them to you. To some He gives a message of wisdom, to another a message of knowledge, and to another great faith. Some will receive gifts of healing, miraculous powers, and prophecy from My Spirit. Others will be able to use great discernment or will have My gifts of speaking in tongues and interpreting tongues. All My gifts are the work of My Holy Spirit. Earnestly desire My Spirit's giftings for you.

DANIEL 4:2–3; ACTS 2:17–21; 1 CORINTHIANS 12:1–11

Prayer Declaration

Father, fill me with Your Holy Spirit, and count me worthy to be filled with the power to perform signs, wonders, and miracles in Your name. Your power will confound and defeat all the powers of darkness and will cause many to desire Your salvation. Your power is awesome and mighty to overcome all the works of the devil.

YOU WILL OVERCOME THE DEVIL BY THE BLOOD OF MY SON

JUST AS THE blood of a lamb, sprinkled on the doorposts in Egypt by My chosen people, established a covenant of blood with Me and protected them from the destruction that I brought to those who had enslaved them, so too have I established a covenant of blood with you. Through the blood of My dear Son, Jesus, that covers you, I have redeemed you from the curse of sin and have adopted you as My own dear daughter. I have equipped you with everything good for doing My will, and I will work in you to cause you to do what is pleasing to Me. Through the blood of Christ you can have confidence to come into My presence. In His blood I have given you redemption, forgiveness of sins, and have redeemed you from the power of evil.

EXODUS 12; HEBREWS 13:20–21;
REVELATION 12:10–11

Prayer Declaration

I have eternal redemption through the power of the blood of Christ. I have been raised to new life in Christ so that I may serve the living God. I overcome the devil through the blood of Jesus. Through Him I am made perfect and have the confidence to enter into the presence of God.

THE BLOOD OF MY SON WILL GIVE YOU PEACE

MY GRACE, MERCY, and peace are yours through the great work of My Son, Jesus, and the sacrifice of His blood on the cross. Come to Me, and I will teach you to fear My name. Turn from evil and do good; seek peace and pursue it. Remember the promise of My Son to give you the Holy Spirit to teach you all things and to remind you of everything He had taught you. My Son has given you peace, which is yours through His Holy Spirit. It is not the kind of peace the world gives, so do not allow your heart to be troubled and filled with fear. Allow your mind to be controlled by My Spirit, for then you will have life and peace.

COLOSSIANS 1:17, 10; PSALMS 34:11–14; 37:37;
JOHN 14:25–26

Prayer Declaration

Through Your precious blood, Jesus, You have reconciled me to Yourself, and have filled me with life and peace. No longer am I ruled by the evil control of Satan, but through the blood of Jesus I have been presented holy in Your sight. Through the blood of Christ, equip me to be pleasing to You, and to do Your will in my daily life.

THE BLOOD OF MY SON BREAKS THE POWER OF SIN AND INIQUITY

I AM LIGHT, and in Me there is no darkness at all. You cannot walk in darkness and have fellowship with Me. But the blood of My Son, Jesus, has purified you from all sin and enabled you to walk in My light and to have fellowship with Me. Trust in My Son's sacrifice of blood, for if you will confess your sins, I will be faithful and just and will forgive all your sins and purify you from all unrighteousness. Do not fear what the accuser of My daughters can do to you. For you have been given the power to triumph over him through the blood of the Lamb and by the word of your testimony. Hold fast to your testimony about the power in the blood of My Son, Jesus.

HEBREWS 10:19–22; 1 JOHN 1:5–7;
REVELATION 12:10–12

Prayer Declaration

I have boldness to enter into Your presence through the blood of Your Son. I have received deliverance through Your blood, and it gives me victory. I rebuke Satan, the accuser of the brethren, through the blood of Jesus. I command all my accusers to depart, and I rebuke and cast out all spirits of slander and accusation.

MARCH

Learning to Battle
With Authority

I Will Teach Your Hands to War

When My people in Israel repented from their evil ways and cried out to Me, I raised up Othniel, Caleb's younger brother, to be a deliverer for them. With My power he overcame their enemies and brought peace to the people. Just as I raised up Othniel, I will raise you up to make war against your enemies. I will teach your hands for war and your fingers for battle. I will be with you like a mighty warrior so that your persecutors will stumble and not prevail. You will see My vengeance against your enemies, for I have committed My cause to you. I have placed My weapons of war in your hands, and I Myself will fight with You. I am the Lord Almighty, and I am mustering an army for war.

Psalm 144:1; Judges 3:9–11; Isaiah 13:4

Prayer Declaration

You are the Lord All-Powerful, and You are bringing together an army for battle. You have prepared Your people to fight with You against wickedness upon the earth. You have filled me with power to fight with You and to declare the return of justice and righteousness to Your people.

WITH MY WEAPONS YOU WILL
DESTROY STRONGHOLDS

DAUGHTER, YOU ARE My mighty warrior. You are living on the earth, but you do not fight your battles with the weapons of this world. Instead, you use My power, which can destroy any fortresses of evil. You have been trained for war and equipped with My weapons so that you can destroy the evil imaginations of this world and every bit of worldly knowledge that would keep people from obeying Me. In My strength you will break through all the enemy's walls and reduce his strongholds to ruins. You will turn back his sword and put an end to his splendor and cast his throne to the ground. You will cut off the nations and demolish their strongholds. Their streets will be left deserted, and no one will pass through their land.

2 CORINTHIANS 10:3–5; PSALMS 89:40, 43–44

Prayer Declaration

Deliver me from my strong enemy, from them that are too strong for me. I am Your battle-ax and weapon of war. I am Your anointed, and You give me great deliverance. I am Your end-time warrior. Use me as Your weapon against the enemy.

I Will Deliver You From Your Enemies

I WILL SHOW Myself faithful to the faithful and blameless to the blameless. I will save the humble but bring low those whose eyes are haughty. I will keep your lamp burning and turn your darkness into light. With My help you can advance against a troop and scale the protective wall of your enemy. I am the God who arms you with strength and keeps your way secure. I make your feet like the feet of a deer and will provide a broad path for your feet. You will pursue your enemies and overtake them. You will crush them under your feet, and they will not be able to rise. I am the God who avenges you and subdues nations under your feet.

PSALM 18

Prayer Declaration

The Lord lives! Praise be to my Rock! Exalted be God my Savior! He is the God who avenges me, who subdues nations under my feet. He has exalted me above my foes and rescued me from violent men. He gives His king great victories and shows His unfailing love to His anointed.

YOU WILL PURSUE YOUR ENEMIES AND OVERTAKE THEM

MY PRECIOUS DAUGHTER, you do not need to be filled with terror and fear when your enemies plot against you and pursue you. Trust instead in Me, for indeed I am Your God, and your times are indeed in My hands. In the shelter of My presence you are hidden from your enemies and from the intrigues of evil men. Do not be afraid of your enemies. I have given them into your hand. Not one of them will be able to withstand you. But don't stop—*pursue your enemies.* Attack them from the rear, for I, the Lord your God, have given them into your hand. I will remove your enemies from your land just as I would remove savage beasts, and the sword will not pass through your country.

PSALM 31:14–15, 20; JOSHUA 10:8, 19;
LEVITICUS 26:6–8

Prayer Declaration

I trust You, Lord. I celebrate and shout because You are kind. You saw all my suffering, and You cared for me. You kept me from the hands of my enemies, and You set me free. I will praise You, Lord, for showing great kindness when I was like a city under attack. You answered my prayer when I shouted for help.

LEARNING TO BATTLE WITH AUTHORITY   67

YOU WILL DESTROY ALL ANIMALISTIC DEMONS

Do NOT FEAR when the enemy comes after you disguised in the animalistic characteristics of wild beasts and dangerous vipers. If you fight in My power and strength, you will tread on the lion and the cobra, and you will trample the great lion and the serpent. The wild boars from the forest will not be able to ravage you, nor will insects from the field be able to feed on you. I will protect you from the prowling of beast in the darkness, when lions roar for their prey and seek their food. Though the leopard lies in wait near your home to tear to pieces those who venture out, it will not do you harm, for My power in you is greater than all the power of the enemy.

PSALMS 91:13; 104:2–21; JEREMIAH 5:6; LUKE 10:19

Prayer Declaration

I tread upon serpents and scorpions and over all the power of the enemy, and nothing shall by any means hurt me. I tread down the wicked; they are ashes under my feet. I rebuke every spirit that creeps forth from the forest. In the name of Jesus I close the door to every demonic rat that would attempt to come into my life.

YOU WILL DEFEAT THE ENEMIES OF YOUR FINANCES

I HAVE PROMISED that I will defend My daughters and keep them from harm. I will strike your enemies with great panic, and they will seize each other by the hand and attack one another. The wealth of all your surrounding enemies will be collected—great quantities of silver and gold and material possessions—and will be given to My daughters. Blessed is the one fears Me and finds great delight in My commands. Your children will be mighty in the land, and your generations will be blessed. Honor Me with the wealth that I give to you, and your barns will be filled to overflowing. My blessing upon you brings wealth, and I will add no trouble to it.

ZECHARIAH 14:13–14; PSALM 112:2–3; JOHN 10:10

Prayer Declaration

In the name of Jesus I bind and cast out every thief that would try to steal my finances. The Lord will rebuild the finances of His people and give the treasures of the nations to them. I will not put my hope in my wealth, but I will place my hope in God, who richly has provided me with everything for my enjoyment. I will lay up treasure for myself in heaven and take hold of life eternal.

No Enemy Will Be Able to Steal Your Joy

Because you love My name and rejoice in Me, you will take refuge in Me and will be glad. I will cause you to sing for joy as I spread My protection over you. I will bless My righteous servant and will surround you with My favor. I will make known to you the path of life and will fill you with joy in My presence and with eternal pleasures at My right hand. I will be your strength and your shield. I will be your shepherd and carry you forever. I will turn your wailing into dancing and will remove your sackcloth and clothe you with My joy.

Psalms 5:11–12; 16:11; 126:5–6

Prayer Declaration

In the name of Jesus I bind and cast out any spirit that would try to steal my joy. I will shout to God with cries of joy. How awesome is the Lord Most High, the great King over all the earth. You have restored to me the joy of my salvation and have filled me with Your spirit. Therefore I will joyfully teach transgressors Your ways and will declare Your praise.

You Will Cast Out Any Familiar Spirits

Do NOT COMPLY when someone tells you to consult mediums and spiritists who whisper and mutter. Should not My daughters inquire instead of Me, for I am Your God? Why consult the dead on behalf of the living? Consult My instructions and heed this warning: if anyone does not speak according to My Word, they have no light of dawn. I have given you the power over unclean, familiar spirits, to cast them out, and to heal all kinds of sickness and all kinds of disease. Behold I give you the authority to trample on serpents and scorpions and over all the power of the enemy, and nothing shall by any means hurt you. Nevertheless do not rejoice in this, that the spirits are subject to you, but rather rejoice because your name is written in heaven.

ISAIAH 8:19–20; MATTHEW 10:1; LUKE 10:19–20

Prayer Declaration

In the name of Jesus I bind and cast out all familiar spirits that would try to operate in my life. I bind and rebuke devils in high places in the name of Jesus. Let every spirit hiding from me be exposed in the name of Jesus. Just as Jesus cast out the spirits with a word, so He has given me the authority to do the same.

You Will Command the Enemy to Leave Your Children Alone

Don't ever doubt My power over the enemy who would pull your children into a stronghold of evil. I am able to deliver your children out of the hand of the enemy. Even if your sons and your daughters are taken prey, place your hope in Me, My daughter, and you will not be disappointed. I have given unto you the keys of My kingdom. Whatsoever you bind on earth will be bound in heaven; whatsoever you loose on earth will be loosed in heaven. Your children are a heritage from Me, and the fruit of your womb is your reward for faithfulness. Therefore I will hedge up their way with thorns and make a wall, that the enemy cannot find their paths.

Isaiah 49:22–25; Matthew 16:19; Mark 10:14–16

Prayer Declaration

I command all devils to leave my children alone in the name of Jesus. My children are a heritage from the Lord, and they have been redeemed from every curse. I and the children whom the Lord has given me are for signs and wonders about God. He has established His covenant between me and my seed in all their generations, to be a God unto them and to their seed.

NO DEMONIC SPIRIT WILL STEAL YOUR DESTINY

I WILL FOIL the plans of the nations and thwart the purposes of the peoples, but My plans will stand firm forever, and the purposes of My heart will be fulfilled through all generations. I know the plans I have for you, plans to prosper you and not to harm you, plans to give you hope and a future. Be strong and very courageous. Do not turn from My Word to the right or to the left, that you may be successful wherever you go. Meditate on My Word day and night, so that you may be careful to do everything in it. Then you will be prosperous and successful. I have determined your destiny; who can thwart My plan for you? I have stretched out My hand in the way you should go; who can turn it back?

PSALMS 33:10–11; 16:3; JEREMIAH 29:11; ISAIAH 14:27

Prayer Declaration

I bind and rebuke any spirit that has been assigned to abort my destiny. God will give me strength to bring forth my destiny. I will do the will of God wholeheartedly, serving the Lord, not man. The world and its desires will pass away, but I will live forever because I do the will of God. He will teach me all His ways.

GREATER AM I IN YOU THAN HE THAT IS IN THE WORLD

I AM THE vine; you are the branches. If you remain in Me and I in you, you will bear much fruit; apart from Me you can do nothing. If you remain in Me and My words remain in you, ask whatever you wish, and it will be done for you. You are no longer controlled by your sinful nature, but by My Spirit, who lives in you. I have raised you up that I might display My power in you and that My name might be proclaimed in all the earth. Keep My words and store up My commands within you. Guard My teachings as the apple of your eye. Bind them on your fingers; write them on the tablet of your heart. Because My power is at work within you, you will be able to do immeasurably more than all you ask or imagine.

JOHN 15:5–7; ROMANS 8:9; 9:17; 1 JOHN 4:4–6

Prayer Declaration

Greater is He that is in me than he that is in the world. God's Spirit dwells in me and has given me life. I am able to do immeasurably more than all I could ask or imagine, according to His power that is at work within me. God will continue to fill me with the knowledge of His will through all the wisdom and understanding that the Spirit gives, so that I may live a life worthy of the Lord and please Him in every way.

YOU WILL BIND AND EXPOSE ALL DEMONS OF FEAR

HEAR MY WORD to you this day: Do not be fainthearted or afraid when you face a spiritual battle with Satan and his army. Do not be terrified or give way to panic before them. For I am the Lord your God, and I am the One who goes with you to fight for you against your enemies and to give you victory. Be strong and courageous. Do not be afraid or terrified, for I will go with you. I will never leave you or forsake you. I am your light and your salvation—whom should you fear? I am the stronghold of your life—of whom should you be afraid?

DEUTERONOMY 20:3–4; PSALM 27:1–3; ROMANS 8:15

Prayer Declaration

I bind and cast our all demons of fear and timidity in the name of Jesus. I bind and cast out any spirit that would try to tear apart my life in any manner. I will not fear the enemy and his demonic attacks to fill my life with fear. God has placed me safely within His arms of shelter, and no one will make me afraid.

YOU WILL DESTROY THE SPIRIT OF BEWITCHMENT

MY DAUGHTER, DO not fear when witches and sorcerers attempt to oppose you and hinder you from doing the work I have given to you to do. Instead of being filled with fear, use the power I gave you to destroy the spirit of bewitchment just as Paul did. Do what Paul did—look straight at the witch and say: "You are a child of the devil and an enemy of everything that is right! You are full of all kinds of deceit and trickery. Will you never stop perverting the right ways of the Lord? Now the hand of the Lord is against you. You are going to be blind, and for a time you will be unable to see the light of the sun." As you stand boldly before the witch, you will destroy the spirit within it. Those who hear your words will be amazed at what happens and will heed your teachings about My Word.

DEUTERONOMY 18:10–12; ACTS 13:8–11, NIV;
MICAH 5:11–15

Prayer Declaration

Lord, do not let me operate in the wrong spirit or become bound by the spirit of witchcraft. I bind the evil powers of bewitchment and destroy those spirits from working among my loved ones. Because of Your power at work within me, witches and sorcerers will confess their evil deeds and will burn their tools of witchcraft publicly and turn to You.

I WILL CLEANSE YOUR LIFE
FROM SECRET FAULTS

MY DAUGHTER, BE aware of the danger of trying to hide your faults or actions from Me, for I see the hidden secrets in your heart. Nothing can be hidden from the light of My presence. You were once darkness, but now you are light in Me. Live as a child of light (for My light consists in all goodness, righteousness, and truth) and find out what pleases Me. Have nothing to do with the fruitless deeds of darkness, but rather expose them. Everything exposed by My light becomes visible, for it is light that makes everything visible. Be very careful how you live—not as unwise by as wise—making the most of every opportunity, because the days are evil.

PSALM 19:12–13; JEREMIAH 23:24; EPHESIANS 5:8–16

Prayer Declaration

Lord, cleanse my life from secret faults. I renounce secret and shameful ways. I will not use deception, nor will I distort the Word of God. The only thing that I will hide in my heart is the Word of God, so that I might not sin against You.

I WILL TEACH YOU TO DO MY WILL

I WILL GUIDE you always; I will satisfy your needs in a sun-scorched land and will strengthen your frame. You will be like a well-watered garden, like a spring whose waters never fail. You will raise up the age-old foundations and will be called Repairer of Broken Walls, Restorer of Streets with Dwellings. I will instruct you and teach you in the way you should go; I will counsel you with My loving eye on you. Do not throw away your confidence in My will, for it will be richly rewarded. Continue with perseverance, for when you have done My will, you will receive what I have promised unto you.

ISAIAH 58:11–12; PSALMS 31:1–4; 32:8; 1 JOHN 2:17

Prayer Declaration

Lead me and guide me for Your name's sake. Guide me into all truth. Lead me in a plain path because of my enemies. Make your way straight before My eyes, and make the crooked places straight and the rough places smooth before me. Help me to stand firm in all Your will, mature and fully assured. Teach me to do Your will, for You are my God; may Your Spirit lead me on level ground.

I WILL COVER YOU IN THE GARMENT OF RIGHTEOUSNESS

YOU ARE MY beloved daughter. I have clothed you with garments of salvation and arrayed you in a robe of righteousness. My Holy Spirit has clothed you with power from on high, and you are clothed with My Son, Christ. I have given you My beauty for your ashes, the oil of My joy for your mourning, and My garment of praise for your spirit of heaviness. My righteousness is a breastplate of protection for you, and I have shod your feet with the gospel of My peace. I have made you My ambassador, so that you may speak boldly to explain the mysteries of My gospel.

ISAIAH 61:10; EZEKIEL 16:8–13; GALATIANS 3:27;
EPHESIANS 6:14

Prayer Declaration

I am clothed with the garment of salvation. My God has placed the robe of His righteousness over me and given me the garment of praise for the spirit of heaviness. He has prepared me for battle by preparing me with armor of defense. His righteousness is my strong and impenetrable breastplate, and His justice protects me like armor.

YOU WILL UPROOT ANY ROOTS OF WICKEDNESS FROM YOUR LIFE

TAKE HEED TO walk in the way of goodness and keep to the paths of righteousness. For My upright and blameless daughters will dwell in My land. But the wicked will be cut off from the earth, and the unfaithful will be uprooted from it. I have this day given you My authority and power over the nations and over the kingdoms, to root out and to pull down, to destroy and to throw down, to build and to plant. My ax is already at the root of the trees, and every tree that does not produce good fruit will be cut down and thrown into the fire. But if your roots are holy, so will be your branches. When I grafted you into the true vine, which is My Son, you now share in the nourishing sap from the olive root. But remember this: you do not support the root; My Son, Jesus, is the root who supports you.

JEREMIAH 1:10; ROMANS 11:17–19; HEBREWS 12:15

Prayer Declaration

I lay the ax to the root of every evil tree in my life. Let every ungodly generational taproot be cut and pulled out of my bloodline in the name of Jesus. Let the roots of wickedness be as rottenness. I speak to every evil tree to be uprooted and cast into the sea. Let every root of bitterness be cut from my life. Let Your holy fire burn up every ungodly root in the name of Jesus.

YOU WILL DEFEAT THE SPIRITS OF PRIDE AND REBELLION

Do NOT LET your hearts become filled with pride, for to the proud I will surely unleash My judgment. If you hang on to your pride, I will make you small among the nations; you will be utterly despised. The pride of your heart has deceived you, you who say to yourself, "Who can bring me down to the ground?" Though you soar like the eagle and make your nest among the stars, from there I will bring you down. But My humble daughters will defeat the spirit of pride, and I will be their deliverer.

PROVERBS 15:25; 16:18; PSALM 17:11; ISAIAH 1:20

Prayer Declaration

Lord, let me be clothed with humility. Let all spirits rooted in pride or rebellion come out in the name of Jesus. To fear the Lord is to hate evil, and therefore I hate pride and arrogance, evil behavior, and perverse speech. I will walk in the way of righteousness along the paths of justice. I will clothe myself with humility toward others because God opposes the proud but gives grace to the humble.

YOU WILL COMMAND MOUNTAINS TO BE REMOVED

IF YOU HAVE faith in My power at work in your life, you will be able to command any mountain that rises up against Me or My power in you to fall into the sea. Stand firm in your faith, for many will say in their hearts that they want to ascend to heaven. They will try to establish their throne above the tops of the clouds so that they may be like the Most High. But with My power at work in you, you will bring them down to the depths of the pit. In the last days the mountain of My holy temple will be established as chief among the mountains; it will be raised above the hills, and all nations will stream to it. Many peoples will come and say, "Come, let us go up to the mountain of the Lord. He will teach us His ways, so that we may walk in His paths."

PSALM 65; MATTHEW 21:21–22

Prayer Declaration

I speak to every mountain in my life and command it to be removed and cast into the sea. I speak to every financial mountain to be removed from my life in Jesus's name. Let every evil mountain hear the voice of the Lord and be removed. Let the mountains tremble at the presence of God. Lord, You are against every destroying mountain. Make waste the evil mountains in my life, O Lord.

YOU WILL BIND THE ENEMY AND STRIP HIM OF HIS POWER

WHEN MY SON sent seventy-two of His servants out two by two to bring them the good news of the gospel, they returned in joyful surprise that even demons submitted to them when they used His name. So do not be surprised that I have given you the power to bind the enemy and strip him of his power. He was already stripped of his power in heaven, and I saw him fall like lightning from heaven. I am sending you to open the eyes of those who are spiritually blind in order to turn them from darkness to light and from the power of Satan to Me. Then I will forgive their sins and give them an inheritance of righteousness.

EXODUS 15:6–7; LUKE 10:17–19; ACTS 26:18

Prayer Declaration

Satan, the Lord rebukes you. Through His power I will bruise Satan under my feet. I bind and rebuke all hindering spirits of Satan in the name of Jesus. I will not be terrified of Satan and his demons when they fight against me, for God Himself is with me and will rescue me. Because of the power of Christ at work within me, I have overcome Satan and have stripped him of his power over me.

YOU WILL SPOIL THOSE WHO ATTEMPT TO SPOIL YOU

WHEN THE EGYPTIANS enslaved My people, they oppressed My people and made their lives bitter with hard labor. They even demanded the death of My people's sons, ruthlessly stealing from them and spoiling their lives with sorrow and want. But behold, I have created the spoiler to wreak havoc on those who attack My daughters. Just as I enabled My people to take the silver and gold of the Egyptians with them when I freed them from their captivity in Egypt, so have I given you the power to spoil those who attempt to spoil you. No weapon forged against you will prevail, for this is the heritage of My daughters. Through My Son you have been given the authority to triumph over the powers and authorities that would threaten to oppress and enslave you.

ISAIAH 54:16–17; EXODUS 12:35–36;
COLOSSIANS 2:13–15

Prayer Declaration

Lead the princes of darkness away spoiled. I bind the enemy, strip him of his armor, and divide his spoils. Lord, You have spoiled principalities and powers. I spoil the enemy and take back his goods in the name of Jesus. The enemy will not spoil me, but he will be spoiled. Let the fortresses of darkness be spoiled in the name of Jesus.

YOU WILL BRUISE SATAN UNDER YOUR FEET

MY DAUGHTER, DO not fear Satan and his demonic angels, for I have already cursed him and stripped him of all his power for his deception in the garden. I have given to you the victory over all his impotent attacks against you. If you fully obey Me and carefully follow all My commands, I will set you high above all nations on the earth—far above all principalities and powers and might and dominion, and every name that is named. I will open the heavens, the storehouse of My bounty, to send rain on your land in season and to bless all the work of your hands.

DEUTERONOMY 28:13; ROMANS 16:19–20;
MALACHI 4:3

Prayer Declaration

Lord, remove Satan's seat from my region, city, and nation. The Sun of Righteousness has arisen with healing in His wings, and in His power I will trample the wicked, and they shall be ashes under the soles of my feet. You have enlarged my path under me, so my feet will not slip; my enemies have fallen under my feet.

You Will Be Sober and Vigilant Against Your Adversary

My daughter, remember that you are not living in darkness, but I have made you aware of the evil schemes of the devil. Stay awake and watchful, for you should not be surprised by anything the enemy may try to do. Because you belong to the day, put on faith and love as a breastplate, and wear the helmet of salvation when you attempt to make war against Satan. With your mind alert and sober, set your hope on the grace that will be revealed to you when My Son returns to bring you home to heaven. Be holy in all you do. Live out your time here as a foreigner. Purify yourself with My holy Word. Resist the devil, and stand firm in your faith.

1 Thessalonians 5:4–11; 1 Peter 1:13–15; 5:8

Prayer Declaration

I am sober and vigilant against my adversary, the devil. I am prepared to be victorious over his evil attacks, and I have armed myself with the breastplate of faith and love and the helmet of salvation. Because of the salvation of Christ, I am able to see the evil schemes and tactics of Satan before they are able to do harm to me or my family. He may cause me to suffer, but he will never be able to overcome me or to take me out of the protection of God, my Father.

THE ENEMY WILL FLEE AT YOUR REBUKE

JUST AS I rebuked Satan and defended My servant Joshua, so too will I defend you, My daughter, and will cause the accusations of the enemy to be harmless to you. I have given you the power to speak to the enemy with rebuke, and you will see him flee from you. I have promised that those who rebuke the wicked will have delight, and a good blessing will come upon them. Follow My instruction and learn to do good; seek justice, rebuke the oppressor, defend the fatherless, and plead for the widow. I will rebuke the devourer for your sake, so that he will not destroy the fruit of your ground, nor shall the vine fail to bear fruit for you in the field.

ZECHARIAH 3:1–2; PROVERBS 24:25; MALACHI 3:11

Prayer Declaration

Satan, the Lord rebukes you. Let the enemy flee at Your rebuke, O Lord. Because the Lord has strengthened me, I will rebuke Satan and cause him to cease from attacking my family and me. I will speak to the storm of my life and say, "Quiet! Be still!"

YOU WILL REBUKE ALL WINDS AND STORMS OF THE ENEMY

MY DAUGHTER, DO not fear the enemy, for he will not keep Me from doing the things that I have planned and promised to do since the world began. I have destroyed the fortress of your enemies and will leave their dwelling place in ruins. I will be a place of safety for the poor and needy in times of trouble. When brutal enemies pound you like a heavy rain, I am your shelter. I will keep your enemies from singing songs of victory. I am a powerful yet patient God, and you will be able to see My hand at work in the storms and whirlwinds the enemy brings into your life. Stand in My strength, and in My power face the enemy and rebuke the winds and storms that he attempts to throw at you. I am your protector and your strength, and in My might you will be victorious.

MARK 4:37–39; ISAIAH 25:1–5; NAHUM 1:2–5

Prayer Declaration

God is my place of safety in times of trouble. He is my shelter when brutal demonic storms flood over my soul. At His command, the storms will cease, and Satan will be powerless to harm me. In the power of my God, I will rebuke Satan and will turn away the whirlwinds before they are able to defeat me.

NO DOCTRINE OF THE DEVIL WILL BE ESTABLISHED IN YOUR LIFE

MY DAUGHTER, UNTIL I come, devote yourself to the preaching and teaching and reading of My Word. Do not neglect the giftings I have given to you, and be diligent in all spiritual matters. Watch your life and doctrine carefully; persevere in them. For if you do these things, no doctrine of the devil will be established in your life. My Word is God-breathed and will teach you, rebuke you from error, correct you, and train you in righteousness, so that you may be My servant, thoroughly equipped for every good work. Do not fear the devil, for I will soon crush Satan under your feet.

EPHESIANS 4:14–16; 2 TIMOTHY 3:16–17;
ROMANS 16:17–20

Prayer Declaration

Father, I thank You for warning me to beware of the evil doctrines of the devil. Because of Your righteousness, I have been trained in righteousness, and Satan cannot deceive my mind. In Your power I will reject every false wind of doctrine, the evil trickery of men and demons, and the craftiness of Satan's deceitful plotting to destroy my soul.

YOU WILL WALK IN MY SPIRIT OF EXCELLENCE

You will know that I, the Lord, am your Savior and your Redeemer, the Mighty One of Jacob. The sun shall no longer be your light by day, nor for brightness shall the moon give light to you; but I will be to you an everlasting light and your glory. Though you may be hard-pressed on every side, you will not be crushed. When you are perplexed, I will not forsake you. If you are struck down, you will not be destroyed. By faith you will know that just as I raised up My Son, Jesus, I will also raise you up with Jesus and will bring you before My throne in heaven. Therefore, do not lose heart. For your light affliction, which is but for a moment, is working for you a far more eternal victory. Do not look on the things that you see, but look at those things that are not seen.

ISAIAH 60:1, 15–16; 2 CORINTHIANS 4:7–18

Prayer Declaration

Because the Spirit of God is at work within me, I am empowered to walk in the excellence of God. When troubling and perplexing circumstances come into my life, I will not lose heart. I will not look at things as they are seen, but I will look at the unseen power of God. I will place my eyes on my Father's throne in heaven, and as I walk in His excellence, His Spirit will enable me to radiate His glory.

YOU WILL EXPOSE FALSE MINISTRIES IN MY NAME

WATCH OUT FOR false prophets. They come to you in sheep's clothing, but inwardly they are ferocious wolves. By their fruit you will recognize them. Evaluate them carefully according to My Word, and in My power expose those who are false and who preach deceiving words to My daughters. My true servants have entered with Me into a covenant of life and peace, and they revere Me and stand in awe of My name. True instruction is in their mouths, and nothing false will be found on their lips. They will walk with me in peace and uprightness and will turn many from sin. Heed My words, and serve Me in purity of heart.

MATTHEW 7:15–23; MALACHI 2:5–6; 2 PETER 2:1–3

Prayer Declaration

Let all false ministries that have rooted themselves in my city be plucked up. Let any evil person planted in my church be rooted out in the name of Jesus. I will serve You in purity of heart and will revere Your name. Bind me in a covenant of life and peace with You, O God. Let nothing false be found on my lips. My innermost desire is that You will find me worthy to preach Your Word and thereby turn many away from their sin.

I WILL GIVE YOU BOLDNESS TO PREACH THE GOSPEL

MY DAUGHTER, I have heard the cry of your heart and have seen your faithfulness to Me. Therefore I have answered your cry and have emboldened you to preach My Word. I am sending you out to proclaim My gospel. Heal the sick, raise the dead, cleanse the lepers, drive out demons. Freely you have received, freely give. I am sending you out like sheep among wolves. Therefore be as shrewd as snakes and as innocent as doves. Go into all the world and preach the gospel to all creation. In My name you will drive out demons; you will speak in a new tongue; you will place your hands on sick people and they will get well. I have caused My light to shine in your heart to give you the light of the knowledge of My glory.

2 CORINTHIANS 3:4–5; MATTHEW 10:16;
2 CORINTHIANS 4:6

Prayer Declaration

Because I have been clothed in the righteousness of God Himself, I have confidence and boldness to preach His Word. I will be as bold as a lion and will make known the mystery of the gospel of God. I will preach and teach with a demonstration of the Spirit and of power. May the fire of God be in my tongue to preach and to prophesy.

I Will Guide You Continually

I WILL BE your hiding place, and I will protect you from trouble. I will instruct you and teach you in the way you should go; I will counsel you with My loving eye on you. I will always guide you and provide good things to eat when you are in the desert. I will make you healthy. You will be like a garden that has plenty of water or like a stream that never runs dry. I will clear a path in your desert and will make a straight road for you to follow. I am able to fill in every valley you face and to flatten every hill and mountain that seem to hinder your way. I will level the rough and rugged ground so that all may see that My glory surrounds your path.

PSALM 32:7–8; ISAIAH 58:11; ISAIAH 40:1–4

Prayer Declaration

Father, guide me continually with Your eye. Guide me by the skillfulness of Your hands. Lead me in a plain path because of my enemies. Make the crooked places straight and the rough places smooth before me. Send out Your light and truth, and let them lead me. Teach me to do Your will, and lead me into the land of uprightness.

I WILL MAKE THE CROOKED STRAIGHT AND THE DARKNESS LIGHT

My daughter, I have taken hold of your hand and will guide you. Hold firmly to My Word, for it is the message that gives life. Encourage My people and give them comfort. I selected and sent you to bring light and My promise of hope to the nations. You will give sight to the blind; you will set prisoners free from dark dungeons. I will lead the blind on roads they have never known; I will guide them on paths they have never traveled. Their road is dark and rough, but I will give light to keep them from stumbling.

PSALM 43:3–4; ISAIAH 40:1–4; 42:16–17

Prayer Declaration

Lead me, and make Your way straight before my eyes. Make darkness light before me and crooked things straight. Teach me to light the way for the blind and to bring hope to the nations. Give me the treasure of darkness and Your riches, which are stored in secret places. Strengthen me so that men may know there is none beside You. You came to reveal the true light that gives light to every man who comes into the world.

APRIL

Confronting the
Enemy's Tactics

PREPARE TO CONFRONT THE ENEMY'S TACTICS

My DAUGHTER, DO not be ignorant of the devil's tactics. The devil is a schemer, and he sets traps or snares for My children. But I will give you the power to overcome all of his schemes. Fix your eyes upon Me, for I am your Sovereign Lord. Do not be deceived by Satan's lies. He was a murderer from the beginning, not holding to the truth, for he is a liar and the father of lies. Be aware that in these times there are some who will abandon the faith and follow deceiving spirits and things taught by demons. Follow closely after My Word, for everything I created is good, and you should receive it with thanksgiving.

EPHESIANS 6:10–12; PSALM 140:8–10;
1 TIMOTHY 4:1–4

Prayer Declaration

Lord, arise in me and scatter Your enemies. Cause my evil foes to flee before You. As wax melts before the fire, may Satan's evil schemes perish before You. You have given me Your shield of victory, and Your right hand sustains me. I pursued my enemies and overtook them. I did not turn back till they were destroyed. You are the God who avenges me and saves me from my enemies.

SATAN IS A LIAR AND THE FATHER OF LIES

DON'T ALLOW THE enemy to strategize against you. Overcome and destroy his strategies through prayer. The main tactic of the enemy is deception. He is a liar and the father of lies. My Word will expose his tactics to you. I am light, and My Word is light. The light exposes the enemy and tears away the darkness. Beware of the hosts of lying and deceiving spirits that work under the authority of Satan. These spirits cause delusion, deception, lying, seducing, blinding, error, and guile. Call upon My name, and I will strip away the power from these deceiving spirits and will cause your eyes to be opened. Pray that your enemies will be scattered, confused, exposed, and destroyed.

JOHN 8:44–47; 1 TIMOTHY 4:1; PSALM 68:1

Prayer Declaration

The Lord has rescued me from all my enemies and from the lying and deceiving spirits that belong to the devil. My enemies are destroyed by my God. The Lord will lead me on level ground and will preserve my life. In His righteousness He has brought me out of trouble. With His unfailing love He has silenced my enemies and destroyed all my foes. In His power I will contend with the powers of darkness that are set against the kingdom of God.

BEWARE OF SATAN'S HOST OF LYING AND DECEIVING SPIRITS

My DAUGHTER, SUBMIT yourself to Me, and resist the devil, and he will flee from you. Be self-controlled and alert. Your enemy the devil prowls around like a roaring lion looking for someone to devour. Resist him and stand firm in the faith. Remember that you do not struggle against flesh and blood or natural enemies. Satan masquerades as an angel of light and will cause your enemies to try to destroy My light in your life. Rebuke him in My power and authority, and instruct him to stay away from you.

JAMES 4:7; 1 PETER 5:8; 2 CORINTHIANS 11:14; MATTHEW 4:10

Prayer Declaration

Away from me, Satan! For I will worship the Lord my God and serve Him only. Get behind me, Satan! You are a stumbling block to me; you do not have in mind the things of God, but the things of men. My Lord has given me the authority to trample on snakes and scorpions and to over-come all the power of the enemy. Nothing will harm me.

LEARN THE WARFARE PRAYERS OF KING DAVID

I AM YOUR rock, your fortress, and your deliverer. Take refuge in Me, and I will be your shield and your stronghold. When you call upon Me, I will save you from your enemies. I will reach down from on high and take hold of you. I will draw you out of deep waters and rescue you from powerful enemies and from your foes who are too strong for you. I will be your support and will bring you out into a spacious place because I delight in you.

PSALM 18

Prayer Declaration

The Lord lives! Praise be to my rock! Exalted be God my Savior! He is the God who avenges me, who subdues nations under me, who saves me from my enemies. Therefore I will praise You, Lord, and will sing the praises of Your name. You are my rock, my fortress, and my deliverer.

YOUR VICTORIES OVER SATAN
WILL RELEASE PEACE

MY DAUGHTER, I will give you rest from all your enemies. I will give peace and quietness to all My children. When your ways please Me, I will make even your enemies to be at peace with you. I will give strength to you, and I will bless you with peace. Your salvation will come from Me, and I will be your strength in the time of trouble. I will help you and deliver you and save you because you trust in Me. Do not forget My law, and let your heart keep My commands, for length of days, long life, and peace will be added to you. Trust in Me and lean not on your own understanding; in all your ways acknowledge Me, and I will direct your paths.

PROVERBS 17:7; PSALMS 29:11; 37:35–40

Prayer Declaration

Father, I trust in You with all my heart, and I acknowledge You in all my ways. I will not depart from You or become wise in my own eyes. I will fear Your name and depart from evil, for in so doing I will find health for my flesh and strength for my bones. Your kindness will not depart from me, nor will Your covenant of peace be removed from my life. Great will be the peace of my children and grandchildren.

YOU ARE REDEEMED FROM THE CURSE THROUGH THE POWER OF MY SON

DAUGHTER, YOU ARE My mighty warrior, and I have given you My armor that you may be able to be victorious over the enemy. Use My shield of faith, for with it you will be able to put out all the flaming darts that Satan will try to use against you. Be strong and courageous, for the enemy desires to destroy you altogether. When Leviathan stands before you with sparks of fire spewing from his mouth and smoke going out of nostrils like a boiling pot or a forest fire, you will have the power to utterly defeat him. You will be able to quench every burning light that he uses to try to inflict his destruction upon you. In the name of My Son, Jesus, you will be able to rebuke every firebrand sent against your life.

EPHESIANS 6:13, 16; JOB 41:20–21; ISAIAH 7:4

Prayer Declaration

In Your power, Lord, I quench with the shield of faith every fiery dart the enemy sends my way. In the name of Jesus I quench the darts of jealousy, envy, anger, bitterness, and rage sent against my life. I bind and cast out every fiery serpent sent against me, and I will not be burned by the fire of the enemy.

The Wicked Will Be Destroyed by the Fire of God

I will avenge the attack of the enemy against My righteous daughters with the fire of My vengeance. I will rain down coals of fire and brimstone against the wicked. When you walk through the enemy's fire, you will not be burned, and the flame of the enemy's attack will not scorch you. I will kindle My fire in you, and it shall devour all the dryness that comes into your life. All your enemies will see that I have kindled it, and it shall not be quenched. My devouring fire will go before you, and the flame of My righteousness will burn behind you.

Psalm 140:10; Isaiah 43:2;
Ezekiel 20:47–48; Joel 2:3

Prayer Declaration

I will not fear the enemy's flames or run when the enemy attacks. My Lord will rain down the fire of His vengeance upon them. He will place His holy flame of righteousness within my heart, and it will devour all dry and useless places within me. It will go before and behind me, and it shall never be quenched.

THE ENEMY'S FLAME WILL NOT KINDLE UPON YOU

WHEN YOU WALK through the fire, you shall not be burned, nor shall the flame scorch you. For I am the Lord your God. Fear not the evil threats of the wicked, for just as the flame consumes the chaff, so will My holy flame burn up their root of rottenness, and their blossom will ascend like dust. Just as the flame of the furnace was unable to harm My servants Shadrach, Meshach, and Abednego, neither shall the wicked fire bring harm to you, My daughter, for I will be with you in the midst of the fire. The fire will have no power to harm your body, and not a hair on your head or your garments will be touched by the flame of the enemy.

ISAIAH 43:2; 5:24; DANIEL 3

Prayer Declaration

I will have no fear of the scorching flames of the wicked, for the Lord my God will protect me from being burned. In the name of Jesus I will overcome every fire of wickedness sent against my life. The enemy will not be able to burn up my harvest, and in Jesus's name I quench every torch the enemy would use against my life.

YOU ARE REDEEMED FROM THE CURSE THROUGH THE BLOOD OF JESUS

YOU ARE THE seed of Abraham, and I have redeemed you from the curse through the blood of My Son, Jesus. I have given you blessing instead of cursing, and life instead of death. I will break and release you from all generational curses and iniquities that came as a result of the sins of your ancestors. I have broken all curses of witchcraft, sorcery, and divination against you through the power of My Son. I will break and rebuke all curses of sickness and infirmity in My Son's name. You have been redeemed—you are set free.

GALATIANS 3:13–14; DEUTERONOMY 11:26

Prayer Declaration

I choose blessing instead of cursing, and life instead of death. The blood of Jesus Christ has redeemed me from the curse. No longer will I fear the curse of the enemy, for I have been set free by the power of Jesus Christ.

BREAK THE CURSE OF WITCHCRAFT AND SORCERY

MY DAUGHTER, I have loved you with an everlasting love, and because I love you, I have turned the curses of witchcraft and sorcery from the enemy into a blessing for you. I will help you according to My mercy, that you may know that it was by My hand that I have blessed what the enemy has cursed in your life. I will stand at your right hand and save you from those who condemn you. You will be a blessing to those among whom you were cursed. I am determined to do good to you and your household. Do not fear. But speak the truth to your neighbor, and give truth, justice, and peace to all you meet.

PSALM 109:28–31; ZECHARIAH 8:13–16

Prayer Declaration

Father, in Your name, I break and release myself from all spoken curses and negative words spoken against me by others, and I bless them. No evil curses of witchcraft or sorcery will have any effect upon my life, for You have broken the curse and have turned it into a blessing for my life through Your precious Son, Jesus.

APRIL 11

BE RELEASED FROM THE CURSE OF SICKNESS AND INFIRMITY

Do NOT FEAR that you have been inflicted with a curse of sickness and infirmity, for just as My Son went about healing all kinds of sickness and disease, so have I broken the curse of sickness from your life. I have given you power over unclean spirits, to cast them out, and to heal all kinds of sickness and all kinds of diseases. I have given you My promise to bring health and healing to you, and to heal you and reveal to you an abundance of peace and truth. I will seek that which was lost, bring again that which was driven away, bind up that which was broken, and strengthen that which was sick.

MATTHEW 4:23; 10:1 JEREMIAH 33:6; EZEKIEL 34:16

Prayer Declaration

Father, You are my Great Physician, and You have promised to bind up my broken body and to strengthen me when I am sick. You have released me from the curse of death and destruction and have freed me from all curses of sickness and infirmity in the name of Your Son, Jesus. You have blessed my life and filled me with the blessing of good health.

I Have Given You Power to Release Yourself From the Curse of Lust and Perversion

My daughter, I have given you the gift of My Holy Spirit, who is powerful and strong and who will save you from the curse of lust and perversion that has affected the generations with whom you dwell. Trust My Holy Spirit to give you the power to release yourself from the spirits of lust and perversion. Keep your heart with all diligence, for out of it spring the issues of life. Let perverse lips be far from you, and let your eyes look straight ahead. Ponder the path of your feet, and let all your ways be established. Do not turn to the right or the left, and keep your foot removed from evil.

PHILIPPIANS 2:15; PROVERBS 4:23–27

Prayer Declaration

Holy Spirit, fill me with the power to set myself free from all lust and perversion. I will no longer live under the curse of a perverse heart, and I commit to You today to keep my lips free from perversion and my eyes looking straight at You. Let all my ways be established in righteousness, and continue giving me the strength to remove my feet from all evil.

I HAVE LOOSED YOU FROM SATANIC AND DEMONIC CONSPIRACIES

MY DAUGHTER, REMEMBER My great goodness, which I have laid up for those who fear Me. If you will keep your trust in Me, My goodness will be yours in the presence of the sons of men. I will hide you in the secret place of My presence and will keep you hidden from the evil plots of wicked men. You will be loosed from any evil, demonic conspiracies that the enemy has plotted against you. I have hidden you from their secret plots and from the rebellion of the workers of iniquity who sharpen their tongues like swords and bend their bows to shoot arrows of bitter words at the blameless. I have preserved your life from the fear of the enemy's secret plots.

PSALMS 31:19–20; 64:2–4

Prayer Declaration

Hear my voice, O God, in my meditation; preserve my life from fear of the enemy. Hide me from the secret plots of the wicked, and from the rebellion of the workers of iniquity. Though they talk secretly of laying snares for me and believe they have perfected a shrewd scheme, You will make them stumble over their own tongues, and all who see them will flee far from them. I shall declare Your wonderful works.

LET EVERY STRATEGY OF HELL BE EXPOSED

DO NOT FEAR the strategies of hell that the enemy plans against you, for in the light of My righteousness they will all be exposed. There will be no prospect of success for the evil man, and the lamp of the wicked will be put out. Though the evil one plots against My just daughters and gnashes at them with his wicked teeth, I laugh at him because his day is coming and his own sword will pierce his wicked heart, and I will break his arm from bringing destruction upon you. I will be your stronghold in the day of trouble, for I know those who place their trust in Me.

PSALM 37:12–15; NAHUM 1:7

Prayer Declaration

Father, in the light of Your righteousness, every strategy of hell has been exposed and brought into the light. I am delivered from every satanic trap and plot against me. Let the nets they have hidden catch themselves, and let them fall into the destruction they have plotted for me. Hide me from the secret counsel of the wicked, and divide and scatter those who are joined together against me.

BREAK AND DIVIDE EVERY
DEMONIC CONFEDERACY

I WILL NOT be silent when those who hate me have lifted up their heads and taken crafty counsel against My people. They have consulted together against My daughters and put a confederacy in place to cut you off so that you will be remembered no more. I will deal with them as I dealt with the enemies of the Israelites, and they will become refuse on the earth. They will be like the whirling dust and the chaff that blows before the wind. I will cause them to confounded and dismayed forever, and I will put them to shame that they may perish. For My name alone is the Lord, and I am the Most High over all the earth.

PSALM 83

Prayer Declaration

Father, I break and divide every demonic confederacy against my life in the name of Jesus, and I loose confusion into every demonic confederacy directed against my life, family, and church. Persecute them with Your tempest, and make them afraid of Your terrible storm. Let them be confounded and troubled forever. Let them be confused and attack each other until they perish.

BIND THE PRINCE OF THE POWER OF THE AIR

I HAVE GIVEN you the power to bind the powers of the prince of the power of the air, the spirit who now works in those who are not obedient to My Word. Because of My rich mercy and the great love I have for you, I have made you alive with My Son, Christ, and have saved you with My grace. I have made you to sit together in the heavenly places in Christ Jesus, far above the powers of the prince of the air. Through the name of Jesus I give you the power to bind the powers of darkness that would control the airwaves and would release filth, violence, and witchcraft through the media. My holy fire will burn up all the high places established by the enemy.

EPHESIANS 2:1–7, 6:12; NUMBERS 33:52

Prayer Declaration

Lord, You created the high places for Your glory. Let not the enemy control the high places. In Your name I bind spiritual wickedness in high places, and I pluck down the high places of the enemy. Let the high places of witchcraft be destroyed in the name of Jesus, and let them be purged through Your anointing to become towers of righteousness.

BIND THE POWERS OF DARKNESS THAT CONTROL THE AIRWAVES

MY DAUGHTER, IT is My desire that you will do what is right in My sight and that you will walk in the ways of righteousness. Seek My face, and like My servant Josiah, purge your life and your home of the powers of darkness that arise as altars of wickedness in this present generation. Break down the wickedness of the media, which has corrupted the eyes of this present generation. Take authority over the powers of the enemy that are permeating the airwaves and releasing filth and violence upon this land. Seek My righteousness, and fill the eyes and the ears of this generation with the wonders and miracles of My great love and power.

2 CHRONICLES 34; EPHESIANS 2:2, LEVITICUS 26:30

Prayer Declaration

Lord, I take authority over the princes of media in the name of Jesus. Let the high places of witchcraft be destroyed, and let the eyes and ears of this present generation be turned to Your righteousness. Make me a beacon of light in this evil world, and raise up a standard of righteousness in this land.

ALLOW MY HOLY FIRE TO BURN UP THE HIGH PLACES

IF YOU WILL be like my servant Josiah, whose heart was tender before Me and who humbled himself before Me when I spoke to him of the desolation and curse that would come to those who allow wickedness to dwell in high places, then I will give you peace and keep you from the calamity that will come upon the wicked. Covenant with Me to keep instructions and take a stand for righteousness. Command your people to burn the idols of wickedness that rise up in this land. Do all that you can to see that the evil leaders of wickedness in your nation are brought down out of their high places, and put away those who consult with mediums and spiritists and who lead My people into perversion. I will cause My holy fire to consume their wickedness and will restore righteousness to My people.

2 KINGS 22:19–20; 23:19–24

Prayer Declaration

Lord, let Your holy fire burn up all the high places of wickedness in our land. Purge us from the powers of darkness that invade our airwaves and bring perversion into the hearts of Your people. Cause me to be a firebrand of Your righteousness, and allow me to be a catalyst for a return to Your ways in our land.

MY TRUTH WILL REMOVE EVERY FALSE MINISTRY IN HIGH PLACES

MY DAUGHTER, BE aware that in these days there are false teachers among you who will secretly bring in destructive heresies, even denying the Lord who saved them, and cause many to reject My teachings and My way of truth. Their judgment has been idle for a long time, and because they have grown cold to the truth, they will bring on themselves—and others—My swift destruction. Do not listen to their lies; reject their teachings. They must be removed from their lofty seats of comfort, and the results of their disobedience will become an example to any who might be swayed to follow their ways. Rise up like my servant Josiah; stand for Me in truth, leading all who know you to turn from evil and do what is right in My eyes, not turning aside to the right or to the left.

2 PETER 2:1–3; 2 KINGS 22:1–2

Prayer Declaration

Lord, remove every false ministry and strange god from the high places. Let righteous men with Your wisdom sit in the high governmental places of my city and nation. Let the spiritual foundations that were built in my city, community, and nation be restored. Use me to walk in the spirit of Josiah and lead the people into righteousness.

TAKE POSSESSION OF THE GATE OF THE ENEMY

BECAUSE MY SERVANT Abraham was willing to serve me wholeheartedly, even to the sacrifice of his own son, I established My covenant with him and his descendants for eternity, and I promised that his descendants shall possess the gate of their enemies. This promise is for you and for your descendants. Serve Me with your whole heart, and I will plant your seed in all the nations of the earth, and you and your descendants will possess the gates of their enemies. You will use the battering ram of My holiness to destroy the gates of the enemy and to overthrow the kingdoms of darkness. The gates of hell will have no power to prevail against My daughters, and I will give you the keys of the kingdoms of earth.

GENESIS 22:14–18; EZEKIEL 21:22; MATTHEW 16:18

Prayer Declaration

*Through Your Son, Jesus, let me possess the gate of the enemy.
I release battering rams against the gates of hell, and
they shall not prevail against me. Open to me the gates
of righteousness that I may enter in. Let the gates of
my life and city be open to the King of glory.*

MY HOLY SPIRIT WILL REPAIR THE BROKEN GATES OF YOUR LIFE

RAISE YOUR PRAISES to Me, My daughter, for I have strengthened the bars of your gates and made peace in your borders. Through My Spirit I have made the crooked places straight and broken the enemy's bars of iron from your life. I have opened the double doors of your gates so they will not be shut against Me. I will give you the treasures of darkness and hidden riches of secret places, that you may know that I, the Lord, who call you by your name, am your God. I will establish the gates of praise in your life and open the gates of righteousness that you may enter in.

PSALM 147:13; ISAIAH 45:1–4; PSALM 118:19

Prayer Declaration

Holy Spirit, establish the gates of praise in my life. Repair the broken gates of my life, and open them before me that I may go in and receive the treasure of the hidden riches of Your secret places. Let all the gates of my life and city be repaired through You, and break the gates of brass and iron that the enemy has used to try to hold me captive. Open the double doors of Your righteousness in my life so that the gates will not be shut.

LET THE EAST GATE OF GOD'S GLORY BE REPAIRED

MY DAUGHTER, I will guide you continually and satisfy your soul and strengthen your bones. You shall be like a watered garden and like a spring of water whose waters do not fail. You shall raise up the foundations of many generations, and shall be called the Repairer of the Breach, the Restorer of Streets to Dwell In. Just as My servant Nehemiah repaired the east gate of My house in Jerusalem, so will the east gate in your life be repaired and opened to allow My glory to fill your life. My Holy Spirit will bring restoration to all the gates of your life, and I will come and dwell within your temple in the fullness of My glory.

ISAIAH 45:1–3; EZEKIEL 11:1; NEHEMIAH 1–6

Prayer Declaration

Lord, let the gates of my life and city be repaired through the Holy Spirit. Let the gate of the fountain through which Your Holy Spirit flows be repaired in my life. Let the sheep gate of the apostolic and the fish gate of evangelism be restored. Let the old gate of the move of Your Spirit be repaired and active in this present day. Let the dung gate of deliverance be restored, and let many walk through to their deliverance. Let the water gate in my life allow me to preach and to teach of Your great mercy, love, and salvation.

Let the Fire of God Burn Up Any Idols

Allow My holy fire to burn up and destroy any idol in your life and nation. Through My power I will cause men to throw away their idols and to turn to Me. Renounce all idolatry in your bloodline, and break all curses of idolatry in the name of My Son, Jesus. Stand in My righteousness and join with My servants to abolish all false idols in America and the nations. I will cleanse the land from the pollution of idols and will cause Babylon, the mother of harlots and abominations in the earth, to fall at the name of My Son. Follow My commandment to put no other gods before Me in your life.

Isaiah 31:7; 2 Kings 21:21; Revelation 17:5;
Exodus 20:3

Prayer Declaration

O Lord, let all men throw away their idols and turn to You. I will keep myself from idols and renounce all idolatry and curses from my life through the name of Jesus. Cleanse this land from the pollution of wickedness and idolatry, and allow me to join with Your servants to abolish the idols in America and the nations.

I Will Abolish the Idols in America and the Nations

If My people who are called by My name will humble themselves, and pray and seek My face, and turn from their wicked ways, then I will hear from heaven and will forgive their sin and heal their land. I will hasten the day when I alone shall be exalted in your land, and everything proud and lofty shall be brought low. The loftiness of man shall be bowed down, and I alone will be exalted in that day. I will utterly abolish any false idols, that the glory of My majesty may be seen. My anger will be kindled against the idols that speak delusion and the diviners who envision lies and tell false dreams. I will bring shame upon all idolatry and will strengthen My faithful daughters.

2 Chronicles 7:14; Isaiah 2:11–18;
Zechariah 10:5–6

Prayer Declaration

Lord, cause our nation to humble itself and to pray and seek Your face and to turn from their wicked ways. Forgive our sins and heal our land. Sprinkle this land with clean water, and cleanse us from all filthiness and idols. Let all false gods and idols be removed from the land in the name of Jesus. Let America renounce her uncleanness and enter back into a covenant with You that she will put no other gods before You, O Lord.

DO NOT ALLOW ANYTHING TO TAKE MY PLACE IN YOUR HEART

I AM THE Lord your God, the One who has brought you out of slavery to sin and set you free to serve Me. Do not worship any god except Me. Do not make idols that look like anything in the sky or on earth or in the ocean under the earth. Don't bow down and worship idols. I am the Lord your God, and I demand all your love. If you reject Me, I will punish your families for three or four generations. But if you love Me and obey My laws, I will be kind to your families for thousands of generations. Seek Me, My daughter, and you will find Me if you seek Me with all your heart and with all your soul. I will never forsake you or forget the covenant I made with your fathers. You shall love Me with all your heart and with all your soul, with all your mind and with all your strength.

DEUTERONOMY 5:4–6; MATTHEW 12:30

Prayer Declaration

Lord, You are fearsome; You are the one true God, and I will worship and obey You in the ways that You demand. I will trust completely in You with all my heart and will not lean upon my own understanding. I will acknowledge You in all my ways and allow You to direct me on the paths that I take. Then I will walk safely in all my ways, and my foot will not stumble.

Cast Out the Spirits of Oppression

My Son, Jesus, went about doing good and healing all those oppressed of the devil. Through His name I have given you the power to rebuke and cast out any spirit that would oppress you. Through that power you shall strip all power from any oppressing spirits. I will be your refuge from the oppressor and will deliver you from the wicked who surround you. I have established you in righteousness, and I will keep you far from oppression. I will not allow the enemy to take your inheritance from you through oppression. My daughter, you are My temple, My dwelling place, and I will encamp at my temple to guard it against marauding forces. Never again will an oppressor overrun My people, for now I am keeping watch.

Acts 10:38; Isaiah 54:14; Zechariah 9:8

Prayer Declaration

Lord, You are my refuge from the oppressor. Deliver me from the wicked that would oppress me and from my deadly enemies that would surround me. I rebuke and cast out all spirits of oppression, sorrow, and anything attempting to bring me low in the name of Jesus. I am established in righteousness, and I am far from oppression.

I WILL BE YOUR REFUGE FROM THE OPPRESSOR

MY DAUGHTER, NEVER forget that I am a refuge for you from those who would attempt to oppress you—either from without or from an evil spirit within. I will be your refuge in times of trouble. I will never forsake you when you seek Me and will administer judgment for you because of your uprightness. I am the Lord your God, and I will be with you. I am mighty to save. I take great delight in you, and I will quiet you with My love. I will rejoice over you with singing. I will remove sorrow from you and will deal with all who oppressed you. I will give you honor and praise among all the people of the earth and will restore your fortunes before your very eyes.

PSALM 9:8–10; ZEPHANIAH 3:17–20

Prayer Declaration

Father, You have promised to defend the cause of the weak and fatherless and to maintain the rights of the poor and oppressed. You will rescue the weak and needy and will deliver me from the hand of the wicked that seek to oppress me. You uphold the cause of the oppressed, and You have set me free from oppression.

CAST OUT THE SPIRITS OF AFFLICTION AND SORROW

MY DAUGHTER, I will keep you in perfect peace if your mind is stayed on Me. Trust in Me and seek after Me. I have heard the sighing of your spirit, and I know when your heart pants and your strength fails you. Place your hope in Me, for I will cast out the spirits of affliction and sorrow from your life. Do not be conformed to the cares and problems of this world, but be transformed by renewing your mind in Me, that you may prove My good and acceptable and perfect will for you. Be renewed in the spirit of your mind as you put on the new man of true righteousness and holiness. Set your mind on things above, not on things of the earth. Rest your hope fully in the grace of My Son, Jesus Christ.

PSALM 38:9–10; ROMANS 12:2; EPHESIANS 4:23;
1 PETER 1:13

Prayer Declaration

Father, in Your power I will strip all power from evil spirits that would oppress me. I rebuke and cast out all spirits of poverty. In the name of Jesus I rebuke all spirits of madness and confusion that would attempt to oppress my mind. Through Your power I rebuke and cast out all spirits of affliction and sorrow that would seek to bring me low. The enemy will not take my inheritance through oppression.

I WILL NOT PERMIT THE PROUD TO OPPRESS YOU

I WILL NOT leave you to your oppressors, and I will not let the proud oppress you. I will bless you because you put your trust in Me and do not respect the proud, nor those who turn aside to lies. Meditate on My precepts. Do not fear the oppressors, for I will put them to shame and revive you according to My loving-kindness. I will destroy the house of the proud, but I hear every prayer of the righteous. I will resist the proud, but I will give My grace to you if you remain humble. Behold, I have released you from the oppression of the wicked. I will multiply your life, and you will not be diminished. I will glorify you with My righteousness, and your children will be established. But I will punish all who seek to oppress you.

PSALMS 119:122; 40:4; 119:88; 1 PETER 5:5;
JEREMIAH 30:19–20

Prayer Declaration

Because I have placed my trust in You, O Lord, and have humbled myself and resisted the wicked intentions of the proud, You have blessed my life and set me free from the bondage of oppression. Because of Your loving-kindness to me, I will seek to bring Your consolation and encouragement to others by becoming a servant to them and developing the same attitude as that of Your Son, Christ Jesus.

EXECUTE JUDGMENT AGAINST MY OPPRESSORS

MY DAUGHTER, HEAR my words, for I am the Lord your God. I will execute judgment in the morning and deliver those who have been plundered out of the hand of the oppressor. I will punish them according to the fruit of their doings and will judge them according to My righteousness. I will hold you up in mercy, and in the multitude of the anxieties within you, My comfort will delight your soul. I will seek what was lost and bring back what was driven away. I will bind up the broken and strengthen what was sick. I will make a covenant of peace with you and cause showers of blessing to come down in your season. You will know that I am the Lord who has broken the bands of your yoke and delivered you from the hand of those who oppressed you.

JEREMIAH 21:12; EZEKIEL 34:16, 25–27

Prayer Declaration

Father, because I am Your sheep, You will deliver me from all the places where my oppressors have scattered me. You will feed me in good pasture and shelter me on the high mountains of Your grace. I will no longer be a prey for the wicked but will dwell safely, and no one will make me afraid. For You are my Lord, and You have broken the yoke of oppression and delivered me from my oppressors.

MAY

Recognizing
Demonic Warriors

I HAVE DEFEATED THE PRINCE OF THIS WORLD

MY DAUGHTER, BY His death and resurrection, My Son, Jesus, has made you alive together with Him. He has nailed your sins to His cross. He disarmed all principalities and powers and made a public spectacle of them, triumphing over them. Therefore do not forget that you no longer walk according to the course of this world or according to the demands of the prince of the power of the air. But by the grace of My Son you have been saved through faith, and He has defeated all the powers of the prince of this world from having any effect on your life. Therefore rise up in faith and power, and when the prince of this world attempts to harass you, say, "Sit down, for your rule will collapse, and you will be carried away captive because of the power of my great God in me."

COLOSSIANS 2:15; EPHESIANS 2:2; JEREMIAH 13:18

Prayer Declaration

Jesus, You have cast out the prince of this world and defeated him. You spoiled principalities and made an open show of them. Because of Your great power within me, I bind the power of the air in Your name. I bind the principalities and powers in my region in the name of Jesus, and I command the principalities to come down. The power of God at work in me has made the demands of the prince of this world of no effect in my life.

I HAVE RELEASED MY WARRIOR ANGELS AGAINST DEMONIC PRINCES

WHEN YOU FIND yourself harassed by demonic princes who have come to defeat you and to cause destruction in your life, remember the testimony of My servant Daniel, and My mighty warrior angel who came to fight the prince of Persia in his stead. My warrior angels stand ready to fight for you against the demonic princes in your life. Remember the angel's words to Daniel, for they apply to your life also: "You are greatly beloved by Me. Fear not; peace be to you. Be strong, yes, be strong!" Let the power of my warrior angels, and the words of comfort they will speak to you, touch you with strength, for they stand ready to come to your defense.

DANIEL 10:18–21

Prayer Declaration

Lord, release Your warrior angels against the demonic princes who would try to harass and harm me. Touch my life and strengthen me with Your power. Let Your angels fight the battle in my stead, for in their mighty power the demonic princes of this world will fall in defeat and release me from their grip.

IN MY POWER YOU WILL REBUKE AND BIND THE PRINCES OF DARKNESS

BELOVED DAUGHTER, MEDITATE on My statutes, for they will be your delight and counsel when demonic princes sit and speak against you. When they persecute you without a cause, let your heart rejoice in My Word as one who finds great treasure, because My Word will bring great peace to you and My righteous judgments will keep you from stumbling. My Holy Spirit has given you the power to rebuke and bind the princes of darkness. You do not wrestle against flesh and blood, but against principalities, against powers, against the rulers of the darkness of this age, against spiritual hosts of wickedness in the heavenly places. I am with you, and My power will give you the victory.

PSALM 119:23–24, 161–165; MATTHEW 12:28;

EPHESIANS 6:12

Prayer Declaration

Father, in Your Spirit's power I will bind the prince of the power of the air. I command all principalities of darkness to fall at the name of Jesus. I rebuke and bind all demonic princes that would speak against me and persecute me. I will rejoice in Your Word and in Your promise of great peace and righteous judgment. I cast out Beelzebub and all his demonic princes, and I rise victorious in Your power.

I will Slay the Dragon That Is in the Sea

I have divided the sea with My strength and have slain the dragon that is in the sea. I have broken the head of Leviathan in pieces, and I gave him as meat to those who inhabit the wilderness. I have drawn Leviathan out with a hook and snared his tongue with the line of My judgment. Though there is no one else who is so fierce that he would dare to stir up Leviathan from the deep, yet he cannot stay hidden from My power. My faithfulness will surround you. I rule the raging of the sea, and when its waves rise, I will still them. Do not fear the demonic dragon of the seas—his power is ineffectual over you because I have sought him out and destroyed him.

Isaiah 27:1; Psalm 74:14; Job 41:1–2, 10

Prayer Declaration

O Lord, break the heads of the dragons in the waters. Break the heads of Leviathan in pieces, and break the strength of his neck. Lord, You rule the sea and all that is in it with Your power, and You will not allow the evil waters of the dark to flood over my life.

I Rule the Sea and the Waters by My Strength

I rule the sea and waters by My strength, and I am mightier than the noise of many waters or the mighty waves of the sea. The sea is Mine, for I made it, just as I formed the dry land. When you go down to the sea in ships and do business on great waters, you will see My works and My wonders in the deep. It is I who commands and raises the stormy wind and who lifts up the waves of the sea. I cause them to mount up to the heavens and to go down again to the depths. I will calm the story so that its waves are still and guide you to your desired haven. I will make a way in the sea and a path through the mighty waters.

Psalms 93:4; 107:23–30; Isaiah 43:16

Prayer Declaration

Lord, You rule the sea and the waters by Your strength, and You will not let any evil waters overflow my life. Your power will protect me, and no evil waves will rise up against me, nor will I be cast into the depths of the sea. Just as You dried up the sea and the waters of the great deep to make a road for the Israelites, so too You will make a road through the sea for the redeemed to cross over.

I Have Broken Leviathan's Power From Your Life

My daughter, I have broken the demonic power of the sea serpent from your life. I have caused all his demonic little demon fish to stick to his scales as I brought him up out of the midst of the sea and cast him into the wilderness to lie on the open field as food for all the beasts of the field and the birds of the heavens. The rivers and seas belong to Me, and I will make utterly waste and desolate the places where his evil power has dwelt. I am the One who commands the sea and its streams to run dry, and I have broken the power of the evils of the sea from bringing destruction to your life.

Ezekiel 29:3–5; Isaiah 44:27

Prayer Declaration

Father, in the name of Jesus I bind every sea monster that would attack my life or region. You have raised a watch against Leviathan, and You will not let the demonic powers of the sea oppress me. You have stripped him of his power and have taken away his armor. You have caused the places of his domain to become utterly waste and desolate and have thrown him and his demonic spirits into the wilderness to be food for the beasts and birds who dwell there.

IN THE NAME OF MY SON YOU WILL DRY UP THE SEAS OF DEMONIC POWER

Do NOT FEAR the sea or the demonic spirits that dwell there, for I am the One who commands the sea and its streams to run dry. I will turn rivers into a wilderness, and the watersprings into dry ground. I will cause the dry land to spring forth into watersprings and make a place for you to dwell. I have come to cause waters to burst forth in the wilderness and streams in the desert. The parched ground shall become a pool, and the thirsty land springs of water. My highway of holiness shall be there, and you will walk on My road, for you are My redeemed daughter. Everlasting joy will be on your head, and you will find joy and gladness as all your sorrow and sighing flee away.

PSALM 107:35–37; ISAIAH 35:6–10

Prayer Declaration

Father, You have dried up the rivers and seas that the enemy brought into my life to bring me to destruction. You have opened the waters of the deep and destroyed the enemy's threats against me. You have established Your highway of holiness and have set my feet upon it. I will be found there, and I will walk with You in joy and gladness as Your ransomed daughter.

I HAVE LOOSED THE HOUNDS OF HEAVEN AGAINST JEZEBEL

MY DAUGHTER, DO not fear the evil powers of the spirit of Jezebel, for I have loosed the hounds of heaven against her. Just as I raised My faithful servant Jehu to bring destruction to evil Queen Jezebel, so I have given you the power to destroy the power of the spirits of Jezebel from your life. Because of My power at work in you, you will rebuke and bind the spirits of witchcraft, lust, seduction, intimidation, idolatry, and whoredom, which are connected to this evil spirit. Arise in the spirit of Jehu, and use My power to defeat the evil Jezebel spirits from your life and the lives of your loved ones.

1 KINGS 21:23; 2 KINGS 9:30–37

Prayer Declaration

Father, I take command over the spirits of witchcraft that are at work through the evil spirit of Jezebel, and I rebuke it from my life. I will not fear the evil plans of the Jezebel spirit to entrap me or the members of my family with the bondage of witchcraft in any form. Greater is the power of my God within me than the evil intents and schemes of the devil and his spirits of Jezebel.

You Will Rebuke All the Powers of Jezebel Out of Your Life

My daughter, place yourself securely within the control and power of My Holy Spirit so that you will not be surprised or intimidated by the overwhelming of the spirit of Jezebel in your world today. Allow My presence to permeate your spirit and sensitize you to all the gateways by which the devil and Jezebel may enter your life. Get rid of the gods of Jezebel who creep in unawares into your home. Do not let the diviners and evil prophets of this world deceive you, nor listen to the lies they would tell you about your thoughts and dreams. Watch out for the evil influence of this world's enchanters, astrologers, and diviners. Allow the power of My Holy Spirit to fill your life with My power, which alone is mighty enough to destroy the spirits of Jezebel out of your life.

1 Samuel 28:9; Jeremiah 29:8; Daniel 5:11

Prayer Declaration

Father, I loose tribulation against the kingdom of Jezebel. I rebuke and tear down her strongholds, and in the name of Jesus and the power of the Holy Spirit I destroy her witchcraft. No longer will she be allowed to cast spells or influence me or my family to practice idolatry. Greater is the power of Your Holy Spirit within me than the evil power of Jezebel upon me.

MY POWER WILL CUT OFF THE ASSIGNMENT
OF JEZEBEL TO CORRUPT THE CHURCH

REMEMBER MY WARNING to the church at Thyatira, and do not allow yourself or your family to be like it. For I know your works, love, service, faith, and patience. But if you allow the evil assignment of Jezebel to corrupt you or My church in this present day, then I will also say to you: Because you allowed the spirit of Jezebel to teach and seduce My daughters to commit sexual immorality or to worship idols, and did not repent, then I will allow sickness and tribulation to enter your life. But if you will hold fast to what I have commanded you, and overcome the evils of Jezebel until I return for you, then I will give you power over the wickedness in this world.

REVELATION 2:18–29

Prayer Declaration

Father, I rebuke all spirits of false teaching, false prophecy, idolatry, and perversion connected with Jezebel. I cut off the assignment of Jezebel against the ministers of God. I will love You wholly, serve You with all the works of my hand, live faithfully according to the instructions of Your Word to me, and hold fast to You until You return.

IN MY POWER YOU WILL BIND AND CAST OUT ALL DESERT SPIRITS

BECAUSE YOU ARE My daughter and have committed your life to Me, I have given you the power to bind and cast out the desert spirits who have taken authority in the spiritually dry desert lands in the hearts of those who live in disobedience to Me. No longer will the desert spirits make their homes in your life or possess the dark regions of your heart to raise their young. I have given you authority and power to cast out these evil desert spirits. The spiritual desert that once possessed you will be gone, and I will bring forth the blessings of My own habitation within your spirit.

ISAIAH 34:11–15

Prayer Declaration

I speak to every desert spirit in my life or ministry in the name of Jesus. I bind and cast out any desert spirit sent against my life. I bind and cast out every spirit of the desert owl, the desert fox, the desert dragon, the desert hyena, and the desert vulture in the name of Jesus. I will not dwell in the wilderness, but in a fruitful land.

You Will Not Dwell in the Wilderness

Just as I brought My children of Israel out of the barren wilderness where they wandered for forty years, so I will not cause you to dwell in a spiritual wilderness any longer. Because you have listened to My words and have honored Me with your life, I will not forsake you in the wilderness, but I will lead you on the road and show you light to bring you out into the land I have promised to you. I will sustain you as you leave the wilderness, and you will have lack of nothing. I will turn your wilderness into a pool of living water and cause My watersprings to rise up out of your dry land. I will establish My dwelling place with you and will bless you, give you a fruitful harvest, and cause you to multiply greatly.

Nehemiah 9:19–21; Psalm 107:35–38

Prayer Declaration

Lord, release Your living water in my dry places and create streams in the desert of my heart. Let Your rivers flow into my desert places. I will not dwell in the wilderness but will be led by You into a fruitful land. My desert shall blossom as a rose and bring forth abundant fruit.

MY RIVERS OF BLESSING WILL FLOW
IN YOUR DESERT PLACES

MY DAUGHTER, I will cause My rivers of blessing to flow in your desert places and will cause your life to be a place of deep rivers and wide streams safe from enemy ships. I will make rivers flow on mountain peaks and will send streams to fill the valleys. Dry and barren land will flow with springs and become a lake of blessing. I will lead you and cause you to walk by the rivers of water in a straight way in which you will not stumble. Behold, My Son will call to you, saying, "If you are thirsting, come to Me and drink. For out of My heart of love for you will flow rivers of living water." If you will drink of the living water from My Son, you will never thirst again. The living waters in you will become a fountain of water springing up into everlasting life.

ISAIAH 33:21; 41:18; JEREMIAH 31:9;
JOHN 7:38; 4:13–14

Prayer Declaration

Father, You have turned my desert places into a pool of living water and have caused Your watersprings to rise up out of my dry ground. Continue to open rivers in high places and fountains in the midst of the valley. Make my wilderness places a spring of living water. I will drink deeply of the living waters that I may never thirst again.

MY POWER WILL CAUSE YOUR DESERT TO BLOOM ANEW

MY POWER WILL fill your desert with all kinds of trees—cedars, acacias, myrtles, olive, and cypress. The firs and pines will burst forth with new life, and everyone will see this and know that I am the God who has redeemed you from the wilderness. I will cause you to be prosperous and to grow like a garden with plenty of water. Wherever this water flows, it will bring life and fresh water to the dead places of your life. Trees of spiritual fruit will grow all along this river and produce fresh spiritual fruit in your life. The fruit of My Spirit will burst forth—My love, joy, peace, forbearance, kindness, goodness, faithfulness, gentleness, and self-control. It will draw many to Me because of the blessing of My new life in your heart.

ISAIAH 41:19; JEREMIAH 31:12; GALATIANS 5:22–23

Prayer Declaration

Father, plant in my life and desert places the trees of new life in You. You have redeemed me from the wilderness and will cause Your spiritual fruit to burst forth in my life. Fill my life with the fruit of Your Spirit, that all who know me will see the fruit of love, joy, peace, forbearance, kindness, goodness, faithfulness, gentleness, and self-control in all that I do. Let me be a blessing to others because of the rivers of blessing and new life that You have given to me.

I HAVE REMOVED DESOLATION
FROM YOUR BLOODLINE

YOU ARE MY beloved daughter, and no longer will you be called *Deserted* or your life be named a place of *desolation*. You will be called My delight, for I have covenanted Myself with you in an everlasting bond. As a bridegroom rejoices over his bride, so will I rejoice over you. As I did for My children in the wilderness, so I will split the rocks in your wilderness and give you water to drink as abundant as the seas. I will bring streams of My living water out of the rocky crags in your desert places and will make water flow down like rivers for you and your generations. I will bring you out of desolation, and My Son will shepherd you and lead you with skillful hands, just as My servant David tended his sheep.

ISAIAH 62:4–5, NIV; PSALM 78:15–16, 70–72

Prayer Declaration

No longer will desolation and dryness cause me to dwell in a spiritual wilderness, for God has made all my wilderness places like Eden and my desert places like the garden of the Lord. Let every desolation in my life or bloodline be raised up in the name of Jesus. Revive me, and repair every desolation in my life.

THE DEMONIC HORSE AND RIDER ARE THROWN INTO THE SEA

SING TO ME, My daughter, as Miriam sang. Exalt My name, for the demonic horse and driver in your life have been hurled into the sea. I will be your strength and your defense. I have become your salvation. I am a warrior, and I will hurl the demonic army that has been coming against you into the sea, just as I did with Pharaoh's chariots and his army. I will shatter the horse and rider and break in pieces the enemy's chariots. I will raise My mighty sword against the enemy and against his horses and chariots, and they will become weaklings that are plundered in the sea.

EXODUS 15:1–2; JEREMIAH 51:21; 50:37

Prayer Declaration

Let the enemy's horse and rider be thrown into the sea. Break in pieces the horse and his rider. Break in pieces the chariot and his rider. I release the sword of the Lord upon the horses and chariots of the enemy's army. They will be destroyed in the sea just as my God's powerful sword destroyed the horses and chariots of Pharaoh because of his vengeance against the people of God.

You Will Overthrow the Enemy's Chariots and Bring Down Their Horses

Just as I spoke to My servant Zerubbabel regarding the restoration of My house from the destruction of the enemy, so too I speak to you, My daughter. Be strong, for I am with you. I have covenanted with you, and My Spirit remains among you. Do not fear. I am going to shake the heavens and the earth, and I have placed My power within you. You will overturn and shatter the power of the enemy. You will overthrow the enemy's chariots and their drivers. Their horses and riders will fall, each by the power of My sword. I will make you like My signet ring, for I have chosen you. You will be an immovable rock, and I will strike every enemy warrior with panic and madness. I will blind the enemy's horses and will keep a watchful eye over you.

Haggai 2:4–5, 21–23; Zechariah 12:4

Prayer Declaration

Overthrow the enemy's chariots and those who ride them. Make the horses afraid as the grasshopper. Smite the horses with astonishment and the riders with madness and blindness. Let the demonic horsemen of the enemy's army fall under their own horses, and let them not be able to rise. Let the chariots and horsemen be burned with Your fire.

I HAVE REMOVED THE STRENGTH OF DEMONIC HORSEMEN

BEHOLD, DO NOT fear the strength of demonic horsemen who come to attack you, for I have removed their strength in the name of My Son, Jesus. You will have My power to render powerless the demonic horsemen who attack you. I have given you My power to bind and rebuke every black horse that would come against you with scarcity and poverty. You will bind and rebuke every red horse that tries to engage you in conflicts and wars with others. You will destroy the power of the pale horse that comes to you with the spirit of death. Through the power of My Son's name you will be victorious over the attack of Satan with his demonic horsemen.

2 SAMUEL 8:2–4; JOB 39:19; REVELATION 6:4–5, 8

Prayer Declaration

Through the power of Jesus Christ, I destroy the strength of any demonic horsemen from my life. In the name of Jesus I bind and rebuke every black horse that would come against me with the spirit of want and poverty. In Jesus's name I bind and rebuke every red horse that would come against me with the spirit of conflict and war. In the name of Jesus I bind and rebuke every pale horse that would come against me with the spirit of widespread death.

I Am the God of the Valleys

MY DAUGHTER, DO not be afraid of the valleys that seem too big for you to conquer, for I am the God of the valleys. Remember My servant Gideon, who faced the host of Midianites who came against him in the valley. Do not try to come against the enemy in your valley experiences in your own strength. Just as the strength of the Midianites was too great for Gideon, so the power of the enemy is too great for you if you fight in your own strength. Do not fear the enemy. You will defeat your enemies just as Gideon did—by obeying My Word and by following My instructions. Pick up your torches and trumpet and declare the victory is yours by, "The sword of the Lord!" I will defeat your valley enemies in My power and will cause your enemies to flee.

JUDGES 7

Prayer Declaration

Lord, You are the God of the valleys, Cast out every valley spirit through the mighty power of Your sword. I will arise in Your power with my torch and my trumpet, and I will declare, "The victory is mine through the power of the sword of the Lord!"

I Will Bless All Your Valley Places

My daughter, when you go through the valley of fear and trouble, lift up your eyes to Me, for I will bless all your valley places. I will meet you in the valley, and I will speak tenderly to you. I will give you back your vineyards and will make your valley experience a door of hope. A fountain of living water will flow from My throne and will water your valley and will bring forth new life. The desert will rejoice and blossom as the rose. I will strengthen your weak hands and make firm your feeble knees. I will restore your strength and will come and save you. Waters shall burst forth in the wilderness and streams in the desert. The parched ground will become a pool, and the thirsty land will become springs of living water.

Hosea 2:14–15; Joel 3:18; Isaiah 35:1–7

Prayer Declaration

Let all my valley places be blessed in the name of Jesus. Open a door of hope in all my valley places. Let water flow into every valley place in my life. Because my God has rescued me, restored my hope, and caused new life to spring forth out of the death of my valley, I will rejoice and will place my feet on His highway of holiness. I will come before Him with singing, with everlasting joy. Sorrow and sighing will flee away, for my Lord has filled me with joy and gladness.

MY RIVER OF BLESSING FLOWS INTO EVERY VALLEY PLACE

MY DAUGHTER, My river of blessing is starting to flow into all your valley places. Lift up your eyes to Me. Do not bow down in your valley experience and lose hope, for I have promised to send My living water to be a fountain of blessing to you. The mountains will drip with the new wine of My Spirit, and a fountain of living water will flow from My throne to water all your valley places. Every valley shall be filled and every mountain and hill brought low. The crooked places will be made straight and the rough ways smooth. You will see the salvation of your God, and you will arise in hope. Though you walk through the valley of the shadow of death, fear no evil, for I am with you. My rod and My staff will comfort you, and I will prepare a table of My blessing in the presence of all your enemies.

JOEL 3:18; LUKE 3:5; PSALM 23:4–5

Prayer Declaration

Lord, I praise Your name for the river of Your blessing that is beginning to flow in my life, filling up all my valley places. I will arise in hope, for I can see the salvation of my Lord flowing into my life. I will no longer fear the darkness and uncertainty of the valley, for even though I have to walk through a valley of death, You will be with me with Your comfort and blessing.

BLESSINGS FROM MY LOVING-KINDNESS

DAUGHTER, I WILL vindicate you, for you have walked in My integrity and have trusted in Me. I will not let you slip. I have examined you and have proven you. I have tried your mind and your heart. My loving-kindness is before you, and you will not sit with the wicked. I will redeem you and be merciful to you. Your foot will stand in an even place, and I will bless you in My congregation. I will set your feet upon a rock and establish your steps. I will put a new song in your mouth, praises to Me, and many will see it and fear and trust in Me.

PSALMS 26:1–1, 11–12; 40:3

Prayer Declaration

I will wait patiently for You, Lord, for You will incline Your ear to my cry. Many are Your wonderful works that You have done. Your thoughts toward me cannot be recounted in order; if I would declare and speak of them, they are more than can be numbered. I delight to do Your will, O my God, and Your law is within my heart.

ASK, AND IT WILL BE GIVEN UNTO YOU

"ASK, AND IT shall be given you; seek, and ye shall find; knock, and it shall be opened unto you: for every one that asketh receiveth; and he that seeketh findeth; and to him that knocketh it shall be opened. Or what man is there of you, whom if his son ask bread, will he give him a stone? Or if he asks for a fish, will he give him a serpent? If ye then, being evil, know how to give good gifts unto your children, how much more shall your Father which is in heaven give good things to them that ask him?" My daughter, if two of you agree on earth concerning anything that you ask, it will be done for you from My throne in heaven.

MATTHEW 7:7–11, KJV

Prayer Declaration

Father, I will give to Your work, and it will be given to me: good measure, pressed down, shaken together, and running over. For with the same measure that I use, it will be measured back to me. If I abide in You and Your words abide in me, I will ask what I desire, and it shall be done for me.

GREAT GOODNESS IS LAID UP IN HEAVEN FOR YOU

I HAVE LAID up My great goodness for you. My goodness will continually be in your life. I will withhold no good thing from you. I will give you that which is good and let you increase. I will show you the path of life. In My presence is fullness of joy, and at My right hand are pleasures forevermore. I will give you life and length of days.

PSALMS 31:19; 52:1; 85:12; 16:11; 21:4

Prayer Declaration

Lord, even with You is the fountain of life, and in Your light I shall see light. Your words will be life to my soul and grace to my spirit. You have redeemed my life from destruction and crowned me with Your love. Let Your blessing fill my life and come upon my family.

YOU WILL EXPERIENCE GREAT BREAKTHROUGH

MY DAUGHTER, I have anointed you for breakthrough. I am the Lord, Your breaker, and I will go before you. I have reconciled you to Myself through My Son and have given you the ministry of reconciliation. Your light will break forth like the morning, and your healing shall spring forth speedily. You will worship Me and sing praises to My name. The end of all things is at hand; therefore break through in your prayers and be ever serious and watchful for Me.

ISAIAH 61:1; MICAH 2:13; 2 CORINTHIANS 5:12;
ISAIAH 58:8; 1 PETER 4:7

Prayer Declaration

Lord, through You I will experience breakthrough in every area of my life. Let me break through in my finances and in all my relationships. Give me a breakthrough in my health with healing. Let me break through to new levels in my praise and worship to You. I will experience a deeper prayer life and will be ever serious and watchful for You to act in my life.

UNDERSTAND THE BLESSING OF OBEDIENCE

DAUGHTER, YOU SHALL love Me with all your heart, with all your soul, with all your strength, and with all your mind. Cast down arguments and every high thing that exalts itself against My knowledge, bringing every thought into captivity to the obedience of My ways. Do not obey unrighteousness, but obey My truth. Then My indignation and wrath will be far away from you. You will receive My blessings because you obey My commandments.

LUKE 10:27; 2 CORINTHIANS 10:5; ROMANS 2:8

Prayer Declaration

God, I will obey You and will trust You with my life. I will love You by keeping Your Word in my heart so that I will not sin against You and risk losing Your favor and blessing, for they are life and breath to me. I pray that You will have confidence in my obedience, knowing that I will do even more than You say.

Obey Me Rather Than Man

Obey God rather than man. Do not let sin reign in your mortal body, or obey it in its lusts. If you obey My voice and keep My covenant, I will be a special treasure to You. Turn to Me when you are in distress; turn to Me and obey My voice. I will not forsake you or destroy you, nor will I forget the covenant that I swore to Your fathers.

Acts 5:29; Romans 6:12; Deuteronomy 4:30–31

Prayer Declaration

I will earnestly obey Your commandments to love You and serve You with all my heart and soul. I will observe and obey all Your words, that it may go well with me and my children after me forever. I will walk after You and will fear You. I will keep Your commandments and obey Your voice. I will serve You and hold fast to You.

UNDERSTAND THE BLESSING OF LEADERSHIP

I CONTROL THE course of world events. I remove kings and set up other kings. I give wisdom to the wise and knowledge to the scholars. You should be subject to the governing authorities, because they have been appointed by Me. Pray, intercede, and give thanks for all men, all kings, and all who are in authority. Daughter, do not be like the dreamers who reject authority and speak evil of dignitaries.

DANIEL 2:21; ROMANS 13:1; 1 TIMOTHY 2:1–2; JUDE 8

Prayer Declaration

Power and might are in Your hands, Lord. It is at Your discretion that people are made great and given strength. I will obey and be submissive to those who rule over me. I will pray, intercede, and give thanks for all men and all who are in authority.

EXPERIENCE THE BLESSING OF SHALOM

SHE WHO WOULD love life and see good days, let her refrain her tongue from evil and her lips from speaking deceit. Let her turn away from evil and do good; let her see peace and pursue it. The wisdom that is from above is first pure, then peaceable, gentle, willing to yield, approachable, full of mercy and good fruits, without partiality and without hypocrisy. Follow peace with all men.

1 PETER 3:10–11; JAMES 3:17; HEBREWS 12:14

Prayer Declaration

Father, blessed (enjoying enviable happiness, spiritually prosperous, with life-joy and satisfaction in Your favor and salvation, regardless of their outward conditions) are the makers and maintainers of peace, for they shall be called the children of God. I will live in peace, I will walk in peace, and I will seek peace.

KNOW THE BLESSINGS OF REDEMPTION

My DAUGHTER, CHRIST is your redemption, and you are the ransomed of the Lord. You are redeemed from destruction, and I have crowned you with loving-kindness and tender mercies. I have redeemed you from pestilence and from all curses of failure and frustration. Do not fear, for your Redeemer will help you. Your Redeemer teaches you to profit and leads you in the way you should go. I have turned away your transgressions and will give you everlasting kindness and mercy.

ISAIAH 35:10; PSALM 103:4; DEUTERONOMY 28:20–21;
ISAIAH 48:17; 54:8

Prayer Declaration

My Redeemer has redeemed me from all my troubles. I will rejoice and sing, for the Lord has redeemed me. I have obtained joy and gladness; sorrow and mourning have left my life, for I am redeemed. I am holy, for I have been redeemed. I am justified freely by Your grace and by the redemption that is in Christ Jesus.

I Will Remove Violence From Your Land

I WILL RESCUE you from evildoers and will protect you from the violent who devise evil plans in their hearts and stir up war every day. I will remove those from your land whose deeds are evil and whose hands are filled with acts of violence. They pursue evil schemes, and acts of violence mark their ways. The way of peace they do not know, and there is no justice in their paths. No one who walks along with them will know peace. But if My people who are called by My name will humble themselves and pray and seek My face and turn from their wicked ways, then I will hear from heaven, and I will forgive their sin and heal their land.

PSALM 140:1–2; ISAIAH 59:6–8; 2 CHRONICLES 7:14

Prayer Declaration

Father, deliver me from all who are violent and bloodthirsty. In the name of Jesus I bind all fear and panic that would come through terrorism. I cut the acts of violence out of the hands of the wicked. Let the assemblies of the violent be exposed and cut off. Let violence be no more in my borders. Call Your people to humble themselves and call upon You, and come and forgive our sin and heal our land.

JUNE

Experiencing
Deliverance

I WILL ANSWER THE CRIES OF MY PEOPLE

I AM A God who loves to deliver My daughters. I delivered the children of Israel over and over again. I brought deliverance to My servant David when he sought Me for his salvation. Just so I will answer your cries when you call upon Me. Look to Me, and I will deliver you from all of your fears. I will save you out of all of your troubles if you will bless Me at all times and let praise to Me be in your mouth continually. My deliverance to you is a sign of My great love and mercy for you. My love will never leave you, and My mercy will be extended to you forever. I will be near to you when your heart is broken and will deliver you out of all of your afflictions. If You place your trust in Me, you will never be condemned.

PSALM 34:1–6, 19–22

Prayer Declaration

I will bless the Lord at all times; His praise shall continually be in my mouth. My soul shall make its boast in the Lord; the humble shall hear of it and be glad. Oh, magnify the Lord with me, and let us exalt His name together. For I sought the Lord, and He heard me, and delivered me from all my fears.

LOOSE YOURSELF FROM DARKNESS

I HAVE GIVEN you the power to loose yourself from any control in darkness. My power and authority in your life will enable you to deliver yourself from the control of the enemy. Follow the instructions of My Word, and awake, awake! Put on your strength and your beautiful garments of salvation, and shake yourself from the dust of the enemy's power. Loose yourself from the bonds the enemy has placed around your neck, and be a captive to the enemy's evil control no longer. I will show Myself faithful to you and will keep your lamp burning. I will turn your darkness into light. Know that with My help you can advance against a troop of the enemy's demons, for I have armed you with strength to be victorious.

ISAIAH 52:1–2; PSALM 18:25, 28–29

Prayer Declaration

The Lord has rewarded me according to His righteousness in me and according to the cleanness of my hands in His sight. He has shown Himself faithful to me. He will keep my lamp burning and will turn my darkness into light. He is my shield, and He arms me with His strength. He gave me His shield of victory, and His right hand sustains me.

CONFESS THE WORD OVER YOUR LIFE

MY DAUGHTER, TAKE spiritual responsibility for your life. Do not depend on everyone else for your spiritual well-being. Confess My Word over your life, and rout the enemy from your life with your prayers to Me. Do not allow self-pity or fear to hold you back. Stir yourself up to offer your prayers to Me, for this is your key to victory. Follow the example of My servant Paul. When the enemy bound him with chains and cast him in prison, he was encouraged to speak My Word more courageously and fearlessly than before. When the enemy tries to discourage you and to defeat you, boldly speak My Word to him, for many will hear your testimony and be drawn to Me. Allow My Word to spread wherever you go, for I have made you a light to bring salvation to the ends of the earth.

PHILIPPIANS 1:14; ACTS 13:46–47

Prayer Declaration

Father, I will experience deliverance and release from the power of Satan as I boldly confess Your Word over my life. My mouth will speak words of wisdom, and the utterance of my heart will give understanding. Touch my lips with Your Spirit as you did Isaiah and Daniel of old, and I will speak the truth of Your Word continually. How sweet are Your words to my taste, sweeter than honey to my mouth. Your Word is a lamp to my feet and a light to my path.

THE BENEFITS OF DELIVERANCE

My DELIVERANCE WILL bring you freedom and joy. Because of My deliverance, you will see My mighty miracles and will experience My supernatural breakthrough in your life. Praise Me with all of your heart, and do not forget all My benefits that come to you with My deliverance. I will forgive all your sins and heal all your diseases. I have redeemed your life from the pit and crowned you with love and compassion. I am compassionate and gracious to you, slow to anger and abounding in love. As high as the heavens are above the earth, so great is My love for those who fear Me. I will be with those who love Me from everlasting to everlasting, and I will give My righteousness to your children's children if they will keep My covenants and remember to obey My precepts.

PSALM 103:2–8, 17–18

Prayer Declaration

Father, may Your glory endure forever, and may You rejoice in the works of my hands. I will never forget all the benefits of Your deliverance to me. I will trust in You, for You are My God. My times are in Your hands. How great is Your goodness, which You have stored up for those who fear You. You will hide me in the shelter of Your presence and keep me safe in Your dwelling place.

EXPERIENCING DELIVERANCE

PRACTICE WARFARE PRAYER

MY DAUGHTER, I am calling you to spiritual warfare against Satan and his demons of destruction. Do not refuse to gird yourself with My armor and open your mouth for deliverance. Come to Me with a heart ready for war! I have trained your hands for war and your fingers for battle. Declare with your mouth that you are ready for war. You do not wage war as the world does, for the weapons you fight with are not the weapons of the world, for I have given you My divine power to demolish strongholds. You will demolish arguments and every pretension that sets itself up against My knowledge. You will take captive every thought to make it obedient to Me. Proclaim with your mouth, "Prepare for war! Rouse the warriors!" Let the weakling say, "I am strong!" Arm yourself for the battle.

PSALM 144:1; JOEL 3:9–10, NIV

Prayer Declaration

The Lord is my light and my salvation, whom shall I fear? The Lord is the stronghold of my life, of whom shall I be afraid? Though an army besiege me, my heart will not fear. Though war break out against me, even then will I be confident. O Lord, the God who avenges, shine forth. I will rise up for You against the wicked and will take a stand for You against evildoers. You have become my fortress and the rock in whom I take refuge.

BE PATIENT IN BELIEVING FOR YOUR BREAKTHROUGH

I HAVE PROMISED to drive out your enemy and those who oppress you little by little. You will not be able to destroy them all at once, for they would become too numerous for you. But I will deliver them over to you and will inflict defeat upon them until they are destroyed. Therefore be patient in waiting and praying for your breakthrough. Do not become weary in praying for others, and do not become discouraged as you wait for your own total deliverance. As your enemies fall and you experience My freedom, follow My Word and grow in your deliverance as you learn to possess your land. Do not become lazy in your spiritual life, but imitate those who through faith and patience inherited what had been promised to them.

DEUTERONOMY 7:21–23; HEBREWS 6:12

Prayer Declaration

Make me like Caleb and Abraham, who kept the promises You had given and waited patiently for what You had promised. Strengthen me according to Your glorious might so that I may have great endurance and patience. Fill me with the knowledge of Your will through all spiritual wisdom and understanding so that I may live a life worthy of You and may please you in every way, bearing fruit in every good word and growing in Your knowledge daily.

I HAVE GIVEN YOU THE BENEFITS OF BINDING AND LOOSING

THE AUTHORITY THAT I gave to My disciples is the same authority that I have given to you. You will be able to drive out evil spirits and to heal disease and sickness. My authority contains the keys to My kingdom, and whatever you bind on earth will be bound in heaven. Whatever you loose on earth will be loosed in heaven. This power to bind is done by My authority. You are set free from the curse of sin—and you have become a slave to Me. Because of this, My daughter, you have received My gift of eternal life and have been given the power to live a life of holiness.

MATTHEW 10:1; 16:19; 18:18; ROMANS 6:22

Prayer Declaration

Father, I have been set free from the law of sin and death through the gift of eternal life from Your Son, Jesus. I bind the works of darkness out of my life. I loose myself from any curse of sin that is present through inheritance, genetics, familiar spirits, spoken curses, and other destroying influence. Your power and authority have loosed me from all these chains, and I have become Your slave and have determined to live a life of holiness.

EXERCISE YOUR LEGAL AUTHORITY IN ME

MY DAUGHTER, DO not be intimidated by the enemy when he tries to tell you that you belong to him and cannot break free. My power at work in Your life has given you legal authority to bind his influence from your life and to loose you from his death grip. My Son, Jesus, was the mediator of a new covenant for you, and His death paid the ransom to set you free from sin. Therefore, live as one set free, but do not use your freedom as a cover-up for evil—live as My servant, bound to Me by the new and better covenant through My Son's death. Through the new covenant I will put My laws in your mind and will write them on your heart. I will be your God, and you will be My daughter. Walk in your legal authority, and do not fear the devil and his works of darkness.

HEBREWS 9:15; 1 PETER 2:15; HEBREWS 8:10

Prayer Declaration

I have been set free from the law of sin and death and from the devil and his works of darkness. I stand in the righteousness of Christ, and I live through the power and authority of the new covenant that God has established with His people. I will walk in my legal authority into a life of holiness and service to my God, and I will never again fear what the enemy might do to me. I am free indeed!

You Will Break Generational Curses in My Strength

The power and authority that I have given you because of the sacrifice of My Son, Jesus, enables you to loose yourself and your loved ones from any curses that have come to you through your inheritance or generations. His power and authority at work in your life will heal the brokenhearted, proclaim liberty to the captives, open the prison for those who are bound, rebuild the old ruins, and repair the desolation of many generations. Just as I gave the rainbow to Noah as a sign that I will remember My everlasting covenant with My children, so too my gift of salvation and deliverance to you through My Son, Jesus, is an everlasting loosing of the bondage of generational curses that had entered your life in times past. Rise up and be encouraged. If My Son has made you free, you are free indeed!

ISAIAH 61:1–4; GENESIS 9:12; JOHN 8:36

Prayer Declaration

Because of the power and authority of Jesus Christ, I break all generational curses of pride, rebellion, lust, poverty, witchcraft, idolatry, death, destruction, failure, sickness, infirmity, fear, and rejection. I command all spirits from my past that are hindering my present and future to come out in the name of Jesus, and I command all ancestral spirits that entered through my ancestors to come out.

I Will Deliver You From Fear

My daughter, I have heard your cries, and I have delivered you from all your fears. I have established My dwelling place within your life, and My love has been perfected in you. Abide in Me, and I will abide in you, just as My Holy Spirit abides in you. I am love, and she who abides in love abides in Me. There is no fear in love, but perfect love casts out fear. Remember that I have not given you a spirit of fear, but of power and of love and of a sound mind.

PSALM 34:4; 1 JOHN 4:15–18; 2 TIMOTHY 1:7

Prayer Declaration

I will bless the Lord at all times; His praise shall continually be in my mouth. My soul shall make its boast in the Lord. I sought the Lord, and He heard me and delivered me from all my fears. I cried out to the Lord, and He heard me and saved me out of all my troubles. Many are my afflictions, but the Lord delivers me out of them all. He redeems my soul, and I have placed my everlasting trust in Him.

I WILL DELIVER YOU FROM UNFORGIVENESS

I DELIGHT IN showing My compassion and mercy to you, My daughter. I have pardoned all your iniquities and do not retain My anger forever. I have promised to cast all your sins into the depths of the sea. I loved you so much that I gave My only begotten Son, that if you only believe in Him, you would not perish but have everlasting life. Therefore, follow My instruction to give the same forgiveness to others that I have given to you. Do not harbor anger, resentment, and bitterness in your heart against another. Do not let a spirit of unforgiveness take control. I have delivered you from the sin of unforgiveness; therefore rise up and comfort those who need you to offer your forgiveness and compassion to them. Reaffirm your love to them, lest Satan should take advantage of you.

MICAH 7:17–18; JOHN 3:16; 2 CORINTHIANS 2:7–10

Prayer Declaration

I have been delivered from the spirit of unforgiveness. I am no longer bound by spirits of pride, hurt, rejection, fear, anger, wrath, sadness, depression, discouragement, grief, bitterness, and unforgiveness against others. I have been set free by the love and mercy of God, who has forgiven all my iniquities and released me to show the spirit of love and mercy to others. I will walk free of unforgiveness from this time forward and will never again be filled with unforgiveness.

I Will Deliver You From Double-Mindedness

My daughter, follow My Word to you through my servant Jude to build yourself up in your most holy faith and to pray in My Holy Spirit. Then your faith will be strong, and you will stand in faith when your faith is tested with the trials and temptations that you face. The testing of your faith produces patience, and through your patience you will become perfect and complete, lacking nothing. Come to Me in total faith, with no doubting, for he who doubts is like a wave of the sea driven and tossed by the wind. I cannot answer the prayers of a double-minded man, for he is unstable in all his ways. If you will stand in faith, I will deliver you from all double-mindedness and will establish you in all your ways.

Jude 20; James 1:1–8

Prayer Declaration

Father, direct my heart into the love of God and into the patience of Christ, that I may be delivered from any double-mindedness regarding the things of God. I stand on the promises of Your Word and commit myself to fight the good fight of faith that I may lay hold of the blessings of God. I will not allow doubt to creep into my life but will wait with faith and patience to inherit Your promises.

I Will Deliver You From Condemnation

I HAVE SPOKEN to you through My Word, affirming to you that there is therefore now no condemnation to those who have accepted the atoning work of My Son, Jesus. You no longer walk according to the flesh but according to My Spirit. The law of the Spirit of life through My Son has set you free from the law of sin and death. Therefore stand firm in your deliverance from condemnation and from all the spirits of guilt, shame, and condemnation that may be attacking you still. Command that they leave! Daughter, if your heart does not condemn you, you will have confidence toward Me and will receive from Me, for you are pleasing in My sight.

ROMANS 8:1–2; 1 JOHN 3:21–22

Prayer Declaration

I command all spirits of guilt, shame, and condemnation to come out of my conscience in the name of Jesus. I have been delivered from all condemnation through the atoning work of Christ, and I will no longer allow the spirit of "what used to be" to inhabit my heart. I am a new creation in Christ; the old has gone, and the new has come!

I Will Deliver You From Pride

I HAVE DELIVERED you from the spirit of pride, for by pride comes nothing but strife. Pride goes before destruction, and a haughty spirit before a fall. It is better that you be lowly in spirit than to boast in your pride. My daughter, this is the one I esteem—she who is humble and contrite in spirit and who trembles at My Word. Follow the example of My Son, Jesus, who was gentle and humble in heart. Be completely humble and gentle; be patient, bearing with one another in love. Make every effort to keep the unity of the Spirit through the bond of peace. Humble yourself to Me, and I will lift you up.

PROVERBS 13:10; MATTHEW 11:29; EPHESIANS 4:2

Prayer Declaration

I command all spirits of pride, stubbornness, disobedience, rebellion, self-will, selfishness, and arrogance to come out of my will in the name of Jesus. Your Word has promised that although You oppose the proud, You will give grace to the humble. I submit myself to You. I will humble myself before You, and You will lift me up.

I Will Deliver You From Witchcraft

My daughter, I have delivered you from the demonic spirits of witchcraft. Do not fear the evils of the occult, for Satan and his demonic witches have no control over your life. The works of the flesh have been loosed from your life through the power in the salvation of My Son, Jesus. I have destroyed idolatry, witchcraft, and all the works of the spirits of the occult from your life, and through My Holy Spirit who resides in you I have created you unto good works. From this time forward you will produce only the fruit of My Spirit and the works of righteousness.

GALATIANS 5:19–22

Prayer Declaration

Father, through the gift of salvation in Your Son, Jesus, You have purchased for me my deliverance from the evil spirits of witchcraft and the occult. I command all spirits of witchcraft, sorcery, divination, and occult to come out in the name of Jesus. I am no longer under Satan's control, and I will no longer produce the acts of the sinful nature in my life. Your Holy Spirit resides in me, and I will produce only the fruit of the Spirit in my life.

I Will Send My Angels to Fight for You

My daughter, because you dwell in the secret place with Me and have turned to Me for your refuge and fortress, I have covered you with My wings. I have given My angels charge over you to keep you in all your ways. In their hands they will bear you up. Just as I sent Michael, My great angel warrior, to defend My servant Daniel, so too I will send My angels to fight for you. I will bring you safely to My holy city of Zion, where an innumerable company of angels will be your defense. I will release My angelic army—thousands of thousands—to defend you. They will destroy the demons that come to destroy you. Fear not, for I will send My angels to minister unto you.

PSALM 91:1–12; HEBREWS 12:22; PSALM 68:17

Prayer Declaration

Let Your angels ascend and descend upon my life. Give Your angels charge over me, and deliver me. Let Your angels fight for me in the heavens against principalities. Let Your angels go before me and make the crooked places straight. I am an heir of salvation, and You will send Your angels to minister unto me in all the circumstances of my life.

JUNE 17

I Will Break the Curse of Poverty

Do NOT WORRY about your life, what you will eat or drink; or about your body, what you will wear. Look at the birds of the air; they do not sow or reap or store away in barns, and yet I feed them. You are more valuable to Me than they, and I know all that you need and desire. Seek My kingdom first, and My righteousness, and all these things will be given to you as well. I have broken the curse of poverty from your life. Blessings and prosperity will be yours, for prosperity is the reward of the righteous. Behold, I have plans to prosper you and not to harm you, plans to give you hope and a future.

MATTHEW 6:25–33; PSALM 128:2; JEREMIAH 29:11

Prayer Declaration

I break all curses of poverty, lack, debt, and failure in the name of Jesus. I seek first the kingdom of God and His righteousness, and all things are added unto me. I break all assignments of the enemy against my finances in the name of Jesus. The blessing of the Lord upon my life makes me rich. Wealth and riches are in my house because I fear God and delight greatly in following His Word. I am God's servant, and He takes pleasure in my prosperity.

I Am Your Jehovah-Jireh

Daughter, I am your *Jehovah-Jireh*—the Lord who provides. Just as I provided the ram to Abraham when he did not withhold his only son from Me, so I will provide all that you need. Follow the example of Abraham, and willingly give to Me all that you are and all that you have so that I may respond in all circumstances as Jehovah-Jireh. The world is mine, and all that is in it. I own the cattle on a thousand hills. I know every bird in the mountains, and the creatures of the field are Mine. Therefore I will meet all your needs according to My never-ending riches.

Genesis 22; Psalm 50:10–12; Philippians 4:19

Prayer Declaration

You are my Jehovah-Jireh, my provider. You are El Shaddai, the God of more than enough. I am blessed coming in and blessed going out because You take pleasure in meeting all my needs. I will freely give You all that I am and all that I have, for You have promised that you will give back to me—good measure, pressed down, shaken together, and running over. Your showers of blessing will cover me, and I will receive more than I have enough room to receive.

TAKE PLEASURE IN MY PROSPERITY

My DAUGHTER, I delight in the well-being of My servants. Because you have freely given Me all you possess—and have faithfully brought your tithes and offerings to Me—I will provide all that you need. Test Me in this, and see if I will not throw open the floodgates of heaven and pour out so much blessing that there will not be room enough to store it. I will prevent pests from devouring your crops, and the vines in your fields will not drop their fruit before it is ripe. I will release the wealth of the wicked into your hands. Your gates will always stand open so that people may bring you the wealth of the nations. Be glad and rejoice, for I have given you abundant showers, and your threshing floors will be filled with grain, and your vats will overflow with new wine and oil.

MALACHI 3:10–11; PROVERBS 13:22;
ISAIAH 60:11; JOEL 2:24

Prayer Declaration

Through Your favor I will be a prosperous person, O Lord. You have called me, and You will make my way prosperous. I am Your servant, and You take pleasure in meeting all my needs. You will release the wealth of the wicked into my hands and will rebuke the devourer for my sake. Let Your showers of blessing flow into my life.

YOU ARE HEALED BY MY STRIPES

MY PRECIOUS SON took up your pain and bore your suffering. He was pierced for your transgressions, and by His stripes you are healed. Because of your faith in My Son, by just one touch of My hand or one word of My mouth you will be healed. I have given to you the same power and authority that My Son had to heal the sick and to raise the dead. I will raise up those who come to Me in faith, for the prayers of a righteous person are powerful and effective. There is healing in the name of My Son, Jesus, from all your infirmities and sicknesses.

ISAIAH 53:4–5; JAMES 5:16

Prayer Declaration

I am healed by the stripes of Jesus. Jesus carried my sickness and infirmities. In the name of Jesus I cast out all spirits of infirmity that would attack my body. I speak healing and strength to my bones, muscles, joints, organs, head, eyes, throat, glands, blood, marrow, lungs, kidneys, liver, spleen, spine, pancreas, eyes, bladder, ears, nose, sinuses, mouth, tongue, and feet in the name of Jesus. I prosper and walk in health even as my soul prospers. I am fearfully and wonderfully made. Let my body function in the wonderful way You designed it to function.

YOU WILL CAST OUT THE SPIRIT OF INFIRMITY

MY DAUGHTER, DO not forget that My Son, Jesus, has given you the power and authority to drive out evil spirits and to heal every disease and sickness. Stand firm in your faith, and cast out the spirit of infirmity that would bring you harm. Just as My Son bore your sins on the cross of Calvary, so too the stripes on His body have made you whole. Take authority over all sickness and death through the name of Jesus.

MATTHEW 10:1; ISAIAH 53:5

Prayer Declaration

I cast out all spirits of infirmity that would attack my body. In the name of Jesus I break, rebuke, and cast out any spirit of cancer that would attempt to establish itself in my lungs, bones, breasts, throat, back, spine, liver, kidneys, pancreas, skin, or stomach. In Jesus's name I rebuke and cast out all spirits causing diabetes, high blood pressure, low blood pressure, heart attack, stroke, kidney failure, leukemia, breathing problems, arthritis, lupus, Alzheimer's, or insomnia. I loose myself from a weakened immune system that is rooted in a broken spirit or broken heart, and I command these spirits to come out in the name of Jesus. Heal and deliver me from all my pains in the name of Jesus.

I Will Make My Grace Abound to You

My daughter, I am able to bless you abundantly, so that in all things at all times, having all that you need, you will abound in every good work. Because I have given you My abundant provision of grace and the gift of righteousness, you will reign in life through My Son, Jesus. I have raised you up with Christ and seated you with Him in the heavenly realms in order to show you the incomparable riches of My grace. For it is by grace that you have been saved, through faith, and this not from yourself—it is My gift to you. Approach My throne of grace with confidence, so that you may receive mercy and find grace to help in your time of need.

2 Corinthians 9:8; Romans 5:17;
Ephesians 2:6–8; Hebrews 4:16

Prayer Declaration

Father, I praise You because You have poured out grace, faith, and love from our Lord, Jesus, on me abundantly. You have justified me freely by Your grace that I might have the hope of eternal life. Your grace and peace will abound to me. Your divine power has given me everything I need for life and godliness. Through Your grace you have given me Your very great and precious promises so that through them I can participate in the divine nature and escape the corruption of this world.

Experiencing Deliverance

I WILL DELIVER YOU FROM EVIL

MY DAUGHTER, DO not forget that My Son has taught you to pray by praying, "Deliver us from evil." I have promised to deliver you from the evil one and to keep you from all evil. Call upon Me in the day of trouble, and I will deliver you. I will deliver the needy who cry out, the afflicted who have no one to help. I will take pity on the weak and the needy and save the needy from death. I will rescue you from oppression and violence, for precious is your blood in My sight. Surely I will deliver you for a good purpose; surely I will make your enemies plead with you in times of disaster and times of distress. I came to deliver you and to crush the leader of the land of wickedness.

PSALMS 50:15; 72:12–14; JEREMIAH 15:11;
HABAKKUK 3:13

Prayer Declaration

*Our Father which art in heaven, hallowed be Thy name.
Thy kingdom come. Thy will be done on earth as it is in
heaven. Give us this day our daily bread. And forgive us
our trespasses as we forgive the trespasses of others. Lead
us not into temptation, but deliver us from evil. For Thine
is the kingdom, and the power, and the glory forever.*

DO NOT BE AFRAID OF EVIL TIDINGS

Do NOT BE afraid of evil tidings, for I have promised that the righteous will never be shaken. They will be remembered forever. They will have no fear of bad news; their hearts are steadfast, trusting in Me. Their hearts are secure; they will have no fear. In the end they will look in triumph on their foes. I will keep you from all harm. I will watch over your life. I will watch over your coming and going both now and forevermore. I have honored the prayer of My Son, who prayed for you by saying, "My prayer is not that You take them out of the world but that You protect them from the evil one." Do not be afraid. You will not be overcome with evil, but you will overcome evil with good.

PSALMS 112:6–8; 121:7–8; JOHN 17:15

Prayer Declaration

Father, because of Your deliverance, I will not be afraid of evil tidings. I will not be visited with evil, for You will preserve me from all evil. Be pleased to save me, Lord; come quickly, Lord, to help me. May all who want to take my life be put to shame and confusion; may all who desire my ruin be turned back in disgrace. For I will seek You and will rejoice and be glad in You because of Your saving help.

RENOUNCE ALL SEXUAL SIN

My DAUGHTER, I urge you to offer your body as a living sacrifice, holy and pleasing to God, for this is your true and proper worship to Me. Do not conform to the pattern of this world, but be transformed by the renewing of your mind. Then you will be able to test and approve what God's will is—His good, pleasing, and perfect will. Flee from sexual immorality, for you are not your own; you were bought at the great price of My Son's death. It is My will that you should be sanctified and avoid all sexual immorality. Learn to control your own body in a way that is holy and honorable. For I did not call you to be impure, but to live a holy life. Put to death, therefore, whatever belongs to your earthly nature—sexual immorality, impurity, lust, and evil desires.

ROMANS 12:1–2; 1 THESSALONIANS 4:3–7;
COLOSSIANS 3:5

Prayer Declaration

Father, I renounce all sexual sin of my past and command all spirits of lust and perversion to come out in the name of Jesus. I release the fire of God to burn out all unclean lust from my life. I receive the spirit of holiness in my life to walk in sexual purity, and I loose myself from the spirit of the world. I overcome the world through the power of the Holy Spirit.

BREAK ALL UNGODLY SOUL TIES

I HAVE CALLED you to come out from among the world, touching no unclean thing, that you might be separate unto Me. Because you have offered your body as a living sacrifice to Me, holy and pleasing and no longer conforming to the pattern of this world, I have given you power and authority to live in holiness before Me. You have been transformed by the renewing of your mind and will be able to test and approve My will for you. Therefore I have given you the power to loose yourself from all ungodly soul ties that have been established by the enemy because of your former sin and impurity. Unrighteousness and holiness have nothing in common, and because you are My daughter, you are no longer bound by the soul ties to sin.

ROMANS 12:1–2; 2 CORINTHIANS 6:14–18

Prayer Declaration

Father, I stand in Your power and authority and loose my spirit from ungodly soul ties the enemy created within me from past relationships of impurity and immorality. I will not be yoked together with wickedness in any form, for I have committed my life to walk in holiness and righteousness. I am crucified with Christ. My old self—a body ruled by sin—has been done away with that I should no longer be a slave to sin. Therefore sin shall no longer reign in my mortal body, for I have become the temple of the living God.

TAKE AUTHORITY OVER YOUR THOUGHTS

My daughter, just as the heavens are higher than the earth, so are My ways—and My thoughts—higher than your thoughts. I am giving you My power to take authority over your own thoughts, that you may grow in My wisdom and knowledge. You have received My Holy Spirit so that you may understand and express spiritual truths in spiritual words, for I have given you the mind of My Son, Jesus. Set your mind on what My Spirit says to you. The mind of sinful man is death, but the mind controlled by the Spirit is life and peace. Take authority over your mind through the power of My Spirit. Think only about those things that are true, noble, right, pure, lovely, admirable, and excellent or praiseworthy.

ISAIAH 55:8–9; 1 CORINTHIANS 2:12–16;
PHILIPPIANS 4:8

Prayer Declaration

I take authority over my thoughts through the power and authority of the Holy Spirit. I will grow and increase in the wisdom and knowledge that come from God. I will focus my thoughts on whatever is true, whatever is noble, whatever is right, whatever is pure, whatever is lovely, whatever is admirable. If anything is admirable or praiseworthy, I will think about those things. And the God of peace will be with me in my spirit and in my mind.

I WILL LOOSE YOU FROM THE SPIRIT OF THIS WORLD

THROUGH MY HOLY Spirit who resides within you, you have been loosed from the spirit of this world. You have received the Spirit of God that you might know the things that I have freely given unto you. When you were controlled by the spirit of the world, you walked in disobedience, gratifying the cravings of your sinful nature and following its desires and thoughts. But because of My great love and mercy for you, I have made you alive with Christ so that I might show you the incomparable riches of My grace. Therefore prepare your mind for action. Be self-controlled, set your hope fully on My grace, and be holy, because I am holy.

1 CORINTHIANS 2:12; EPHESIANS 2:1–7;
1 PETER 1:13–15

Prayer Declaration

Father, I loose myself from the spirit of the world, the lust of the flesh, the lust of the eyes, and the pride of life. I overcome the world through the power of the Holy Spirit. The world and its desires have passed away in my life, and I am committing myself to doing only the will of God who lives within me.

I WILL FREE YOU FROM THE TERROR BY NIGHT

You HAVE BEEN set free from the fear of the terrors that come by night, for you dwell in the shelter of My love. Do not be afraid of the terrors that come from without in the darkness of the night, or of the terrors that come through the demonic visitations of the enemy from within the night. Because you trust in Me, I will be your refuge and your fortress. By the day I will direct My love to you, and at night My song of love will give you peace. I will watch over you. I am your shade at your right hand; the sun will not harm you by day, nor the moon by night. I will keep you from all harm and will watch over your life. I watch over your coming and going and will hide you under the shelter of My wings from all harm.

PSALMS 91:1–2, 5; 42:8; 121:5–8

Prayer Declaration

Father, the day is Yours, and Yours also is the night; therefore I will no longer fear the terror of the darkness. I will praise Your name and proclaim Your love in the morning and Your faithfulness at night. Even the darkness is not dark to You, for in Your presence the night will shine like the day. I am free from the terrors that come in the night because You have become my refuge and fortress, and You have hidden me under the shelter of Your wings.

BIND AND REBUKE THE SPIRIT OF ANTICHRIST

DAUGHTER, YOU HAVE My power and authority to bind and rebuke the spirit of antichrist from your life and your home. Every spirit that does not confess My Son, Jesus Christ, as Lord is the spirit of antichrist. You have overcome them, because greater is He that is in you than he that is in the world. Be alert and spiritually discerning, for many deceivers have entered into this world who confess not My Son. If you abide in the doctrine of My Son, you will have both My presence and My Son's presence in your life. If any come to you and do not believe in My Son, receive them not into your house, for this is the spirit of antichrist.

1 JOHN 4:3, 2 JOHN 7–10

Prayer Declaration

In the name of Jesus I bind and rebuke all antichrist spirits of hatred and murder that would manifest through terrorism. I bind and rebuke all spirits of antichrist and hatred of Christianity in the name of Jesus. I cast out all religious terrorists who do not proclaim the doctrine of Christ. I will continually be spiritually alert and discerning to prevent the entrance of an antichrist spirit of deception into my life or the lives of my loved ones.

JULY

Contending for the
Freedom of Captives

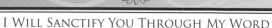

I Will Sanctify You Through My Word

THOUGH THE WORLD hates you, I have taken you out of the world and will protect you from the evil one. You are not of the world, just as My Son was not of the world. I will sanctify you by My truth, for My Word is truth. Sing unto Me with a new song, for My Word is right, and all My works are done in truth. By My Word I created the heavens and the earth and all those who dwell on the earth. I spoke, and it was done. My Word works effectually in you, for it is truth. Therefore My Word is God-breathed and is useful for teaching, rebuking, correcting, and training in righteousness, so that you may be thoroughly equipped for every good work.

JOHN 17:14–17; PSALM 33:4–9; 2 TIMOTHY 3:16

Prayer Declaration

Father, sanctify me through Your Word of truth. Let Your Word have free course in my life. Through Your Word, I will do my best to present myself to You as one approved, a workman who does not need to be ashamed and who correctly handles Your Word of truth. I desire the pure milk of Your Word that I may grow thereby. Teach me through the strong meat of Your Word, that I may discern both good and evil.

I WILL GIVE YOU THE SPIRIT OF WISDOM AND REVELATION

MY DAUGHTER, I will give you the Spirit of wisdom and revelation so that you may know Me better. I will enlighten the eyes of your heart in order for you to know the hope to which I have called you, the riches of My glorious inheritance for you, and My incomparably great power for all who believe. I will teach you in the way of wisdom and lead you in right paths. My wisdom and knowledge will be the stability of your times and the strength of your salvation. I will establish you according to the revelation of My Word and through the revelation of My Son. Where there is no revelation, the people cast off restraint, but you will be happy because you keep the revelation of My Word.

EPHESIANS 1:17–18; ISAIAH 33:6; PROVERBS 29:18

Prayer Declaration

Give me the spirit of wisdom and revelation in the knowledge of Jesus. Let the eyes of my understanding be enlightened that I might know what is the hope of my calling, what are the riches of the glory of Your inheritance in the saints, and what is the exceeding greatness of Your power toward me. Fill my life with Your wisdom and revelation so that I can rejoice and make known the wonders of Your works.

I WILL CAUSE YOU TO KNOW THE LOVE OF MY SON

I HAVE STRENGTHENED you with power through My spirit in your inner being so that My Son may dwell in your heart through faith. I have rooted and established you in the love and given you My power so that you may grasp how wide and long and high and deep is the love of Christ. Our love surpasses knowledge and has filled to you the measure of fullness in Me. I am able to do immeasurably more than all you could ask or imagine according to My power at work in you. Hold fast to My sound Word through your faith and love in Christ. My daughter, nothing shall separate you from the love of Christ—not tribulation, distress, persecution, famine, nakedness, peril, or sword. Through His love you are more than a conqueror.

EPHESIANS 3:15–19

Prayer Declaration

Let me know the love of Christ, which passes all understanding, that I might be filled with all the fullness of God. Lord, do exceeding abundantly above all I can ask or think, according to Your power, which works in me. Enable me to walk in love, as Christ loved me. For the love of Christ constrains me to be an ambassador for Christ, so that others may also share in His love.

OPEN YOUR MOUTH BOLDLY IN MY NAME

You HAVE BEEN filled with the power and authority of My Son, and you will be empowered to speak the gospel boldly wherever you go just as My Son spoke boldly. You will speak with the boldness of My servant Paul, who spoke boldly in the name of My Son and disputed those who would not listen to the gospel, even when they threatened him with harm and death. The words of your mouth will show forth My righteousness and salvation continually, and you will go in My strength. I have made your mouth like a sharp sword, speaking forth the truth of My Word and speaking boldly against the lies and deceptions of the enemy.

JOHN 7:25; EPHESIANS 6:19; ISAIAH 49:2

Prayer Declaration

Father, let utterance be given unto me that I may open my mouth boldly to make known the mystery of the gospel. You have called me to spread forth the truth of Your Word, and You have made my mouth like a sharpened sword and a polished arrow. Make me Your bold servant, and empower me to proclaim Your truth to a world that needs to know it.

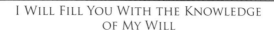

I WILL FILL YOU WITH THE KNOWLEDGE OF MY WILL

My DAUGHTER, I have filled you with the knowledge of My will through the wisdom and understanding that My Spirit has given to you. I have enabled you to live a life worthy of Me—one that will please Me in every way and will bear fruit in every good work as you grow in My knowledge. I have strengthened you with power according to My might, so that you will have great endurance and patience. I have qualified you to share in My inheritance as a member of My kingdom of light. You have been transferred from the dominion of darkness into the kingdom of My Son, and you have redemption and forgiveness of sins through Him.

COLOSSIANS 1:9–14

Prayer Declaration

Father, let me be filled with the knowledge of Your will in all wisdom and spiritual understanding that I may work worthy of You. Make me fruitful in every good work, and increase my knowledge of You.

I Will Preserve You Blameless Before Me

DAUGHTER, ALTHOUGH YOU were once alienated in your mind from Me by your wicked works, I have redeemed You through My Son and have reconciled you through the death of My Son so that you are now holy, blameless, and above reproach in My sight. I will preserve you blameless unto the coming again of My Son. Continue in your faith, grounded and steadfast, not moving away from the hope of My gospel, which you now proclaim. As My steward, you must be blameless, not self-willed or quick-tempered, not drunken, violent, or greedy for the riches of this world. Hold fast to My Word so that you may be able to exhort and convict those who would attempt to contradict the truth of My righteousness.

COLOSSIANS 1:22–23; 1 THESSALONIANS 5:23;
TITUS 1:7

Prayer Declaration

Let my whole soul and body be preserved blameless unto the coming of my Lord Jesus Christ. May I be worthy of being presented in Your sight, holy, without blemish, and free from accusation. Enable me to continue in faith, established and firm, that I may not move from the hope of an eternal life with You.

I WILL COVER YOU WITH MY APOSTOLIC ANOINTING

MY DAUGHTER, I have called you to be My apostle and have covered you with an apostolic anointing. You are appointed a preacher and an apostle to speak the truth in Christ, to be a teacher of the unbelievers in faith and truth. Fix your thoughts on My Son, Jesus, who is the apostle and high priest whom you have confessed and now serve. Be faithful to the one who has appointed you, just as Moses was faithful in My house. Be a builder of My house, but remember that I am the builder of everything. Hold on to your courage and the hope in which you boast.

2 PETER 1:2; 1 TIMOTHY 2:7; HEBREWS 3:1–6

Prayer Declaration

Father, I receive multiplied grace and peace through the apostolic anointing You have given to me. I am Your humble servant, and I will speak the truth in Christ so that unbelievers may know Your love and mercy and become a partaker of Your righteousness. I look to Jesus as my example, and I will faithfully and courageously be a builder of Your kingdom.

I Will Give You the Keys of My Kingdom

My daughter, I have given you the keys to My kingdom. In My power and authority you will be able to bind the power of the enemy and loose the captives from his dominion. You will know the mystery of My kingdom and will bring the glad tidings of My kingdom to those who live in darkness. As I did with My prophet Ezekiel, I am sending you to proclaim My kingdom to a rebellious people that has rebelled against Me. Do not be afraid of them or afraid of their words. Speak My words to them, whether they hear or whether they refuse. Open your mouth, and I will fill it with My Word; receive into your heart all My words, and hear with your ears. And go, get the captives; loose them from the enemy's grip and bring them into My kingdom.

MATTHEW 16:19; EZEKIEL 3:1–11

Prayer Declaration

I have the keys of the kingdom, and whatever I bind on earth is bound in heaven, and whatever I loose on earth is loosed in heaven. I will proclaim the kingdom of God to those to whom the Lord has called me. I will speak of the truth of the Word of God and will loose the captives from the kingdom of darkness.

BIND SPIRITUAL WICKEDNESS IN HIGH PLACES

BE STRONG IN My mighty power and might. Put on My armor so that you can take your stand against the devil's schemes. Your struggle will not be against flesh and blood, but against the rulers, authorities, and powers of this dark world, and against the spiritual forces of evil in the heavenly realms. Therefore I have given you the power to bind the powers of spiritual wickedness in high places. Do not be afraid of the wicked, for they will be brought low by their own wickedness. Because you stand in My righteousness, I will be your deliverer. You have been redeemed from all wickedness by My Son, and He is purifying you as His very own, eager to do what is good. Encourage and rebuke with all authority, and do not let anyone despise you.

EPHESIANS 6:10–12; PROVERBS 11:5–6; ROMANS 1:18;
TITUS 2:13–14

Prayer Declaration

Father, I stand in Your power and authority and bind the principalities, powers, rulers of the darkness of this world, and spiritual wickedness in high places. I love righteousness and hate wickedness, therefore You have anointed me with the oil of joy.

LOOSE THE PRISONERS OF SIN

I AM THE Lord your Maker who stretches out the heavens and who lays the foundations of the earth. Do not live in constant terror every day because of the wrath of the oppressor, Satan, and his demonic forces. He is bent on destruction, but I have given you the power and authority through My Son, Jesus, to loose the prisoners and set them free. They will not die in their dungeon of spiritual darkness. For I am the Lord Your God, the Lord Almighty. I have put My words in your mouth and covered you with the shadow of my hand. Go in My power and strength and set free those who are bound by Satan and his demons.

ISAIAH 51:12–16

Prayer Declaration

Father, loose the prisoners from the captivity and darkness. Fill me with Your power and strength to take the glorious message of Your love and mercy and hope to them. Let them see the salvation of the Lord that has been given to them through the death and resurrection of Your Son, Jesus. Let the exiles be loosed from the bands of wickedness.

I Will Loose Your Mind From the Spirit of Darkness

My daughter, I have come to set free those whom the enemy has bound through the captivity of their minds to spiritual darkness and deepest gloom. You do not need to stumble in your distress, with no one to help. I have heard your cries, and I will save you from your distress and bring you out of darkness and the deepest gloom; I will break away the chains that the enemy has used to take your mind captive. I will be a lamp unto you and will turn your darkness into light. Do not be conformed to this world any longer, but be transformed by the renewing of your mind, that you may prove what is My good and acceptable and perfect will for your life.

Psalm 107:10–14; 2 Samuel 22:29; Romans 12:2

Prayer Declaration

Father, through Your power, I loose my mind, will, and emotions from every assignment and spirit of darkness in the name of Jesus. I will no longer allow the enemy to capture my mind and plunge me into spiritual darkness and deepest gloom. I am no longer conformed to this world and its way of thinking, but by the transformation of my mind I will follow the good and acceptable and perfect will of God.

I WILL LOOSE YOUR CITY FROM THE ASSIGNMENT OF HELL

WHEN MY SON, Jesus, paid the price of redemption from sin through His death and resurrection, He boldly confronted Satan's authority over hell, and He now holds the keys to both heaven and hell. I have given you the power to act in the authority of My Son, and you have the power to bind Satan's authority over your city and to loose your city from the assignment of hell. Do not fear, daughter, but use your authority to loose your city from the enemy's stranglehold. Just as I sent My warrior Michael to defeat the prince of Persia for Daniel, I send him to fight with you. Rise up in My power to loose your city from the principalities, powers, and demonic rulers of wickedness over the heavens.

1 PETER 3:18; REVELATION 1:18; DANIEL 10;
EPHESIANS 6:12

Prayer Declaration

Father, I stand in Your Son's power and authority to confront the demonic powers that have taken my city captive and to loose it from the assignment of hell. Send Your warrior Michael to fight for me, and enable me to set the captives free. I will not be intimidated by the principalities, powers, rulers of the darkness of this age, or the spiritual hosts of wickedness in the heavenly places.

BIND EVIL KINGS AND NOBLES IN CHAINS

My DAUGHTER, I take pleasure in you, for I have beautified you with the salvation of My Son and have robed you with His righteousness. Pick up My two-edged sword and execute vengeance on the demonic forces that have bound nations is darkness. Bind the evil kings with chains, and Satan's demonic nobles with fetters of iron. For I will execute My judgment upon them, just as I have promised in My Word. The intent of their hearts is only evil, and their mouths are filled with lies. But they will not prosper, and they will be defeated through the power and authority I have given to My people. Do not be afraid, for there is no authority greater than Mine, and whoever resists My authority will bring judgment upon themselves.

PSALM 149; DANIEL 11:27–33; ROMANS 13:2

Prayer Declaration

Father, execute Your judgment upon the evil rulers in our world who have fallen under the evil control of Satan. Keep them from prospering and turning the masses of people under their authority to evil. Reveal their evil intentions, and empower Your people to use Your mighty two-edged sword to execute Your vengeance upon these evil demonic forces.

I Will Loose the Bands of Wickedness From Your Land

WHEN I RELEASED My people from their captivity in Egypt, I established a covenant with them. If they would obey Me, I promised to set My tabernacle among them and to break the bands of their yoke and make them to walk upright. I have established the same covenant with My people today. If My people will obey My Word and serve Me with their hearts, I will loose the bands of wickedness from the land. Daughter, I am calling My people to love and obey Me. If they will, I will raise them up, and they will know that I, the Lord, am their God, and that I am with them and they are My people.

LEVITICUS 26:9–13; EZEKIEL 34:30

Prayer Declaration

Father, draw the people of my land to You with gentle cords, with bands of love, and remove the yoke of wickedness from their necks. Do not pour out Your wrath upon us, but raise me up to stand in the gap before You for my land, that it will not be destroyed. Build a hedge of Your protection around this land and keep it safe from the marauding attacks of the forces of evil.

Let the Enemy Be Ashamed

My daughter, I have heard the voice of your weeping and your supplication. I will receive your prayer and will cause your enemies to be ashamed and greatly troubled. I am a God full of compassion and gracious, long-suffering, and abundant in mercy and truth. I have given you My strength and will make you a sign for good, that those who have released their hate upon you will see it and be ashamed. I will help you and comfort you. I will stop those who seek to dishonor you and will turn them back and bring them to confusion. The angel of the Lord will chase them, and their way will be dark and slippery. Therefore be joyful before Me, and rejoice in the salvation I have given to you.

Psalms 6:8–10; 86:15–17; 35:4–9

Prayer Declaration

Father, let my enemies be ashamed and sore vexed. Let them return and be ashamed suddenly. Show me a token for good, that they who hate me may see and be ashamed. Put to shame those who seek after my soul. Let them be confounded and filled with confusion. Fill their faces with shame.

I WILL SHAME THOSE WHO SEEK AFTER YOUR SOUL

I HAVE SEEN the fierce witnesses who rise up and gather together to form an attack against you. I know of those who hate you without a cause and do not speak peace but devise deceitful matters against you. I will vindicate you according to My righteousness. I will let them be ashamed and brought to mutual confusion. Those who rejoice at your hurt will be clothed with shame and dishonor. These workers of iniquity would eat My people as they eat bread. But I despise them, and I will put them to shame and scatter the bones of those who encamp against you.

PSALMS 35:11–27; 53:4–5

Prayer Declaration

Father, put to shame those who seek after my soul. Let them be ashamed and confounded. Let those who desire my hurt be turned backward and put to confusion. Bring me out of my captivity to the enemy, and I will rejoice and be glad in Your great salvation.

LET PROUD SPIRITS BE PUT TO SHAME

MY MERCY IS on those who fear Me from generation to generation. I will show strength to them with My mighty arm and will scatter the proud in the imagination of their hearts. I will put down the mighty from their thrones and exalt the lowly. I will resist the proud, but I give grace to the humble. Because you have hoped in My Word and served Me with a faithful heart, I have extended My merciful kindness for your comfort. I will cause the proud to be ashamed to have treated you wrongfully with their lies.

LUKE 1:50–52; JAMES 4:6; PSALM 119:78

Prayer Declaration

Father, I know that Your judgments are right and that Your tender mercies have given me life. I take delight in Your Word and meditate on Your precepts. Let the proud spirits that rise against me be ashamed. Revive me according to Your loving-kindness so that I may keep the testimony of Your mouth.

I Will Be the Shepherd and Bishop of Your Soul

My daughter, I have established My Son to be the shepherd and bishop of your soul. My Son is the good shepherd who has given His life for the sheep. Listen to His voice, for you will know His voice as the sheep know the voice of their shepherd. Follow Him for He has given you eternal life, and you will never perish, nor will the enemy be able to snatch you out of His hands. He bore your sins in His own body on the tree, that you, having died to sins, might live for righteousness. Once you were like sheep going astray, but now you have returned to the shepherd and overseer of your soul.

John 10:11–16; 1 Peter 2:24–25

Prayer Declaration

Lord, You are the shepherd and bishop of my soul. Watch over my soul and keep it. I will listen to Your voice and will follow Your steps. I will have no fear that the enemy will attack me and snatch me away, for You, the good shepherd, will keep me in the safety of Your fold.

I Will Restore Your Soul

I WILL NEVER leave you alone, but I will keep you safely in the shelter of My sheepfold. I am the good shepherd, and I will bring you into green pastures and cause you to lie down by still waters. I will lead you in the path of righteousness. Fear no evil; I am with You. My rod and staff are Your comfort. I have prepared a table for you in the presence of your enemies. Goodness and mercy will follow you all your days, and you will dwell with Me forever.

PSALM 23, NIV

Prayer Declaration

Lord, You are my shepherd, I shall not be in want. You make me lie down in green pastures; You lead me beside quiet waters, and You restore my soul. You guide me in paths of righteousness for Your name's sake. Even though I walk through the valley of the shadow of death, I will fear no evil, for You are with me; Your rod and Your staff comfort me. You prepare a table before me in the presence of my enemies. You anoint my head with oil; my cup overflows. Surely your goodness and love will follow me all the days of my life, and I will dwell in the house of the Lord forever.

ALLOW MY COMFORTS TO DELIGHT YOUR SOUL

MY DAUGHTER, I will never reject My people or forsake those who are My inheritance. My unfailing love will be your support, and I will comfort your soul when anxiety is great within you. I am your fortress, and I am the rock in whom you take refuge. My Word will give you life and will be the source of your hope. Remember My judgments upon the wicked from My Word, and comfort yourself in My Word. I will comfort you and make your desert places like the garden of the Lord. You will find joy and gladness in Me and will raise your voice in thanksgiving and the voice of melody. I am the God of all comfort who comforts you in trouble so that you may comfort those around you who need My comfort.

PSALM 94:14, 18–19; ISAIAH 51:3;
2 CORINTHIANS 1:3–5

Prayer Declaration

Praise be to the God and Father of our Lord Jesus Christ, the Father of compassion and the God of all comfort, who comforts us in all our troubles, so that we can comfort those in any trouble with the comfort we ourselves receive from God. Our hope for you is firm, because we know that just as you share in our sufferings, so also you share in our comfort.

CONTENDING FOR THE FREEDOM OF THE CAPTIVES   211

POUR OUT YOUR PRAISES TO MY NAME

Do NOT BE downcast, My daughter, and disturbed within yourself. Put your hope in Me, and rise up to praise Me, for I am your Savior and your God. I will bring You back from the enemy to Myself and will cause you to dwell safely. You will be My daughter, and I will be your God. I will give you a heart to fear Me forever and will not depart from you. I will rejoice over you and will do you good and plant you in the land of promise.

JEREMIAH 32:37–41

Prayer Declaration

Praise the Lord, O my soul; all my inmost being, praise His holy name. Praise the Lord, O my soul, and forget not all His benefits—who forgives all your sins and heals all your diseases, who redeems your life from the pit and crowns you with love and compassion, and who satisfies your desires with good things so that your youth is renewed like the eagle's.

I Will Cover You With My Robe of Righteousness

TAKE JOY AND rejoice, My daughter, for I have clothed you with the garments of salvation and covered you with the robe of righteousness. Just as the father welcomed home the prodigal son and brought out the best robe to put on him, so I have welcomed you as My daughter and robed you in the righteousness of My own Son. I have put My ring of approval upon you and have covered your feet with sandals. I have turned your mourning into dancing and have put off your sackcloth and clothed you with gladness. Therefore sing praise to Me and do not be silent. Give thanks to Me forever.

ISAIAH 61:10; LUKE 15:22; PSALM 30:11–12

Prayer Declaration

Father, I praise You because you have clothed me in garments of salvation and covered me with Your robe of righteousness. You have comforted me from my mourning and given me the oil of joy and a garment of praise instead of a spirit of despair. I will delight great in the Lord, and my soul will rejoice in my God.

I Will Bring the Leaders of Your Nation to My Light

ALTHOUGH THE DARKNESS of sin covers the earth and thick darkness is over the peoples, I will rise upon you and My light will shine upon you. Nations will come to My light, and kings to the brightness of My dawn. No longer will the guides in Your nation lead the people astray. No longer will the leaders of My daughters cause them to err, and those who are led by them will no longer be led into destruction. Then My people will sing the song of Deborah: "When the leaders in our nation take the lead, when the people willingly offer themselves, praise the Lord!" By Me kings reign and rulers make laws that are just; by Me princes govern, and all nobles who rule on earth love those who love me, and those who seek Me find Me.

ISAIAH 60:2–3; 9:16; 3:12; JUDGES 5:2;
PROVERBS 8:15–16

Prayer Declaration

Father, I pray for the leaders of my nation to come to Your light. I will make supplication, prayer, intercession, and give thanks for all the people of my nation and for the leaders of my nation that I might live a peaceable life in all godliness and honesty. Let our leaders be just, and let them rule by the fear of the Lord.

MY DOMINION WILL BE ESTABLISHED IN YOUR NATION

MY DAUGHTER, I long to establish My dominion in your nation. Be faithful in your intercession for your nation, that even the kings and rulers from distant shores will recognize that your nation is established upon My precepts and will honor and serve Me also. For when the leaders of your nation are led by Me, I will take pity on the weak and the needy and save them from death. I will rescue My people from oppression and violence, when My people pray to Me and bless My name. The grain will abound in your land, and the crops will thrive like the grass of the field. All nations will be blessed through you and will bless My name.

PSALM 72

Prayer Declaration

Father, endow the leaders of my nation with Your justice and righteousness. Let them judge the people in righteousness. May they defend the afflicted among the people and save the children of the needy. Give them Your strength to crush the oppressor and to endure as long as the sun through all generations. In their days may the righteous flourish and prosperity abound.

I WILL RULE OVER YOUR NATION

MY DAUGHTER, CONTEND diligently for the day when your nation has once again turned to Me and allowed Me rulership over your nation. For then the earth will be glad, and distant shores will rejoice. Righteousness and justice will be the foundation of your nation, and all the people will see My glory. Your nation will love Me and hate evil. I will guard the lives of My faithful ones and deliver them from the hand of the wicked. My light will shine on the righteous, and joy will fill the hearts of the upright. Then you will sing to Me with a new song. You will praise My name and proclaim My salvation day after day. You will declare My glory among the nations, and My marvelous deeds among all peoples.

PSALMS 97; 96:1–3

Prayer Declaration

Lord, rule over my nation, and let my nation be glad and rejoice. Let my nation sing a new song, bless Your name, and show forth Your salvation from day to day. Let our leaders praise You and hear the words of Your mouth. Let the nations proclaim that You reign, and let the world be established firmly in You. Judge the people with equity and righteousness, and reward the people for our faithfulness to You.

I Will Cause the Wicked to Be Rooted Out of Your Land

My daughter, accept My words and store up My commands within you. Turn your ear to wisdom and apply your heart to understanding. Call out for insight. Then you will understand what is right and just and fair—every good path. Discretion will protect you, and understanding will guard you. Then I will save you from the ways of wicked men whose paths are crooked and who are devious in their ways. Thus you will walk in the ways of the good and keep to the paths of the righteous. The upright will live in your land, and the blameless will remain in it. But I will root the wicked out of your land, and the unfaithful will be torn from it.

Proverbs 2

Prayer Declaration

Let the wicked be rooted out of our land. Let them wither like the grass, and like green plants soon die away. Let our nation place their trust in You and do good. Then we will dwell in the land and enjoy safe pasture. Cause us to wait patiently for You. Keep us from fretting when people succeed in their ways and carry out their wicked schemes. For those who are evil will be destroyed, but those who hope in the Lord will inherit the land.

I WILL ESTABLISH RIGHTEOUSNESS
IN YOUR LAND

I WILL ESTABLISH righteousness in your land, and your rulers will rule with justice. Each one will be like a shelter from the wind and a refuge from the storm. Then the eyes of those who see will no longer be closed to Me, or the ears of those who hear refuse to listen. No longer will the fool be called noble, nor the scoundrel be highly respected. My people will live in peaceful dwelling places, in secure homes, in undisturbed places of rest.

ISAIAH 32

Prayer Declaration

I pray that my nation will submit to the rule and reign of Christ. Let those who are deaf hear the words of Your Word, and let the blind see out of obscurity. Rule over our nation in righteousness and judgment. Let Your glory be revealed to my nation so that all the earth will see. Let Your spirit rest upon my nation—the Spirit of wisdom and understanding, the Spirit of counsel and might, the Spirit of the knowledge and fear of the Lord—and our nation will delight in the fear of the Lord.

LET THE CHILDREN OF YOUR NATION BE TAUGHT OF MY GOODNESS

MY DAUGHTER, HEAR the words I spoke to Israel, and know that I would desire the same of your nation at this time. Because of your disobedience to Me, for a brief moment I had hid My face from you. But with deep compassion and everlasting kindness I will bring you back. I will rebuild Your afflicted nation, lashed by storms and not comforted, and will rebuild your foundations and gates. All your children will be taught by Me, and great will be their peace. In righteousness will you be established, and you will have nothing to fear, for tyranny will be far from you. Terror will be removed and will not be able to come near you. This is the heritage of all who serve Me, and this is their vindication from Me.

ISAIAH 54

Prayer Declaration

Father, forgive the disobedience of our nation, and restore our gates and foundations in righteousness. Let the children of our nation be taught of You, and grant to them the heritage of righteousness and peace. Remove tyranny and terror from our land, and release us from the terror of the oppressor.

I Will Be Merciful Unto You and Bless Your Land

When the people of your land have turned back to Me and have committed themselves to righteousness, I will be gracious to you and will bless your land and make My face to shine on you. All your ways will be known on earth, and My salvation toward you will be known among all nations. If you return to Me, then your loved ones and children will be shown My compassion, for I am gracious and compassionate. I will not turn My face from you if you return to Me. I will give you shepherds according to My heart, who will feed you with knowledge and understanding. I will be merciful to your unrighteousness, and your sins and lawless deeds I will remember no more.

Psalm 67:1–2; 2 Chronicles 30:9; Jeremiah 3:15; Hebrews 8:12

Prayer Declaration

Lord, be merciful unto us and bless us, and cause Your face to shine upon us. Let Your way be known to us, and Your saving health in our nation. Let my nation look to You and be saved. Possess our nation as Your inheritance, for the kingdom is Yours, and You are the governor of my nation.

I WILL RAISE UP GODLY LEADERS
IN YOUR LAND

IF YOU TURN to Me in righteousness and integrity, I will raise up godly leaders in your land. In My hand they will have hearts to serve Me and will channel My righteousness to all they lead. They will tremble at My greatness and will praise My great and awesome name. I will speak to them, and they will keep My statutes and decrees. I will answer them when they call to Me, for I am a forgiving God. They will exalt Me and worship at My holy mountain, for I will be their God. There will be no end to the greatness of My government among you, and of My peace there will be no end. I will establish you and uphold you in justice and righteousness from that time on and forever.

PROVERBS 21:1; PSALM 99:1, 8; ISAIAH 9:7

Prayer Declaration

Let the leaders and people who walk in darkness in my nation see the light, and let Your light shine upon those in the shadow of darkness. Let Your government and peace continually increase in my nation. Let Your glory be declared among my people, and Your wonders in my nation. Raise up godly leaders in our land who will lead Your people in integrity and righteousness. May the families of my people be blessed and praise Your great and awesome name.

I WILL POUR OUT MY SPIRIT UPON YOUR LAND

IN THE LAST day I will pour our My Spirit on all people. Your sons and daughters will prophesy, your young men will see visions, and your old men will dream dreams. I will show wonders in the heavens above and signs on the earth below. Everyone who calls on My name will be saved. I will banish the idols from your land, and they will be remembered no more. I will remove both the impure leaders and all impurity from the land. I will pour My Spirit on your descendants and My blessing on your offspring. I will pour My Spirit of grace and supplication upon all your inhabitants, and they will look upon Me and be saved.

ACTS 2:17–21; ZECHARIAH 13:2; ISAIAH 44:3;
ZECHARIAH 12:10

Prayer Declaration

Father, let Your Spirit be poured out on my nation, and let our sons and daughters prophesy. Let righteousness, peace, and joy in the Holy Spirit increase in my nation. Let the families of my people be blessed, and Your Spirit rest on our descendants. Bring Your righteousness and justice to the land, and we will seek Your face and enter into Your rest.

AUGUST

Breaking the
Enemy's Curses

REDEEMED FROM THE CURSE

My DAUGHTER, DO not foolishly try to follow Me by living according the mandates of the law. For I have placed My Spirit within you so that you may live by faith. Remember My Word, which says: "The righteous will live by faith." My Son, Jesus, redeemed you from the curse of the Law by becoming a curse for you. He redeemed you so that by faith you might receive the promise of My Spirit. Before receiving redemption from My Son and learning to walk by faith, the Law was your guardian. But you are no longer under a guardian; through My Son you are a child of God through faith. You have been redeemed from the curse—live no more under the curse of the Law, but live in the righteousness you have received by faith in My Son.

GALATIANS 3

Prayer Declaration

Father, reveal Your righteousness to Me through faith, for it is my desire to live by faith and not by law. I have been crucified with Christ; it is no longer I who live, but Christ who lives in me, and the life that I now live in the flesh I live by faith in the Son of God who loved me and gave Himself for me. Christ has redeemed us from the curse of the law so that I might receive Your blessings through the promise of Your Spirit through faith.

THE RULING SPIRIT OF WICKEDNESS

BE AWARE THAT the wicked and vile spirit of Belial is the ruling spirit of wickedness. He disburses his evil host of demons to curse the lives of people and bring destruction to them. The wicked servants of Belial have arisen among you to lead people astray. When you see wickedness at work among you, investigate it carefully and reveal it for the detestable thing it is. Destroy it completely, and let none of it be found in your hands. If you do this, My daughter, then I will turn from My fierce anger and will show you mercy, have compassion on you, and increase your numbers as I promised to My servant Abraham. I will bless you because you obey Me, and serve Me as Your God, and do what is right in My eyes.

DEUTERONOMY 13:12–18

Prayer Declaration

O God, let our nation fall beneath Your feet, for Your throne will last forever. Let Your scepter of justice arise over us, for You love righteousness and hate wickedness. My mouth will speak what is true, for my lips detest wickedness. I will look to You for wisdom to recognize the wicked works of Belial in our midst. I will dwell with prudence and possess Your knowledge and discretion hating every form of wickedness that I see. I will serve You with my life and do what is right in Your eyes.

AUGUST 3

I Will Rid Your Nation of "Abominations"

My daughter, it is the work of Belial to curse men and women and to cause them to commit sins that are vile and contemptible. His detestable abominations will draw many under the curse of sin and bring My judgment upon them. Keep your eyes on Me, and follow My Word so that you will know that what is highly esteemed among men is often an abomination in My sight. There shall by no means enter into My eternal city anything that defiles or causes an abomination or a lie, but only those who are written in the Lamb's Book of Life.

Proverbs 6:16–19; Luke 16:15; Revelation 21:27

Prayer Declaration

Father, keep me safe from the curse of wickedness. Rid my life of the abominable sins that You hate, and cause me not to think that the highly esteemed things of this world are just. May I be holy and pure that my name may be found in the Lamb's Book of Life and that I may inherit eternal life with You.

I Will Rid You From Worthless Idols

THE WORKS OF wickedness wrought by the evil spirit of Belial draw My daughters away to serve other gods. These gods are worthless idols—good for nothing, vain, of no value, a thing of nought. Have nothing to do with these worthless idols. Remember the sin of Saul, who spared the worthless idols of Agag instead of following My command to destroy them. Because he rejected My words, I rejected him from being king. Turn away your eyes from looking at worthless things, and establish yourself upon My Word. Devote yourself to fearing Me, and I will turn away My reproach from you. Revive yourself in My righteousness.

1 SAMUEL 15; PSALM 119:37–40

Prayer Declaration

Teach me, Lord, the way of Your decrees, that I may follow it to the end. Give me understanding, so that I may keep Your law and obey it with all my heart. Direct me in the path of Your commands, for there I find delight. Turn my heart toward Your statutes and not toward selfish gain. Turn my eyes away from worthless things; preserve my life according to Your Word. How I long for Your precepts! In Your righteousness preserve my life.

I Am Drawing You Back to Worship Me

The wicked spirit of Belial is at work to withdraw the inhabitants of your land from serving God. They lead the people to serve other gods, which removes them from My protection and places bondages upon them that lead to destruction. Beware of this evil spirit, for just as Belial caused the sons of Eli to reject Me and lead many away from Me, so will some wicked religious leaders of today do the same with My people. I am drawing you back to Myself. I desire your worship and long to see you turn back to Me. You are the temple of your living God, and I have promised to dwell in you, and walk in you, and to be your God and you will be My daughter.

Deuteronomy 13:13; 1 Samuel 2:12;
2 Corinthians 6:16–18

Prayer Declaration

Father, give me Your supernatural discernment that I may clearly see those wicked religious leaders in our world who seek to lead Your people away from You to worthless idols of false doctrine and thinking. Draw me back to You, and let me worship You with a clean heart and a life of righteousness. Make me a temple worthy of Your dwelling, and receive me unto Yourself and be my Father.

I Will Take Away Your Apostasy

MY DAUGHTER, My Spirit has clearly spoken unto you to say that in these latter days, some will abandon the faith and follow deceiving spirits and things taught by demons. Do not be seduced by these spirits of apostasy. Do not allow the wickedness of this world to cause you to abandon your loyalty to Me and to lead you to defect from the faith. Have nothing to do with these godless myths and false doctrine. Recognize the absolute value of godliness, and put your hope in Me. Devote yourself to My Word, and do not neglect the gift of My Holy Spirit. Be diligent in these matters, because if you are, you will save both yourself and your hearers from the destruction of an apostate life.

1 TIMOTHY 4

Prayer Declaration

Father, keep Your people from the destructive heresies that cause them to deny You and bring upon themselves swift destruction. These false teachers speak great swelling words of emptiness and allure through the lusts of the flesh. While they promise liberty to their followers, they themselves are the slaves of corruption. I will persevere in Your Word and will not become a victim of apostasy. Remove apostasy from our land, and cause us to turn back to You.

REVEAL THE WORKS OF BELIAL

MY DAUGHTER, KEEP your eyes on Me and on My Word that you may see the revelation of the works of Belial in your world. Arm yourself with the sword of My Spirit to fight this evil spirit. For it cannot be easily pulled up like a thornbush or dug up by hand. It will require the sharp sword of My Spirit to burn it on the spot. Know that the spirit of Belial destroys the godly value that I have given to you and will cause you to become worthless in My sight. Listen only to My Spirit, and I will give you the power and discernment to resist the evil works of Belial from entering your life.

2 SAMUEL 23:6–7; PROVERBS 16:27

Prayer Declaration

Father, help me to recognize the power of Belial and to arm myself with the sword of Your Spirit to fight the evil spirit of Belial. Keep me from trying to find evil in my own strength. Arm me with Your Spirit and strength, and burn evil from my life. May I never become worthless to You. I will not allow the spirit of Belial to destroy my value to You and others.

I Will Rid You From the Curse of Jezebel

REMEMBER MY WARNING to the church of Thyatira, for although I knew everything about them—their love, faith, service, and endurance—still I had one thing against them. They had allowed the evil spirit of Jezebel to teach and seduce My servants to commit sexual immorality and to hunger after idols. Behold I will strike down the evil curse of Jezebel, and everyone who does immoral things with her will be punished. Rid your lives and your nation of the curse of Jezebel. Do not let this evil spirit draw My daughters away from the truth and cause them to go into error, causing bondage and curses and bringing My judgment upon them. Do not allow Jezebel to draw you into whoredom and adultery, for surely this will cause My judgment to come upon you.

REVELATION 2:18–25; HEBREWS 13:4

Prayer Declaration

Father, the spirit of Jezebel is a seducing spirit that is causing rampant destruction in my nation today. Teach me to honor marriage, and guard the sacredness of sexual intimacy between a wife and husband. May I never forget that You draw a firm line against casual and illicit sex. Help us to teach our children the consequences of being unequally yoked in marriage with the evil spirit of Jezebel at work in a person's life.

I Will Restore Your Moral Purity

My daughter, do not allow the evil spirit of Jezebel to cause you to place your trust in your beauty and physical attractiveness and to draw you into immorality. Today your nation is filled with adultery, prostitution, promiscuity, and the false idols of sensuality and lust. Unless you turn back to Me in repentance, you will bear the consequences of your lewdness and detestable practices. Come to Me in repentance, and I will establish My covenant with you and will restore moral purity to your land. Rid your life and your land of the works of the flesh brought on by the spirit of Jezebel, and begin to live by the power of My Spirit and to possess the fruit of the Spirit, which will cause you to crucify the flesh with its passions and desire.

Ezekiel 16; Galatians 5:19–25

Prayer Declaration

Father, the spirit of Jezebel has led our nation into rampant sexual immorality. We have fallen prey to this wicked spirit, and our nation is filled with people who no longer live in purity. Cause Your daughters to make a stand for purity, Lord. Let us lead this nation to repent for its immorality and to turn to You in purity and dedication.

I WILL DEFEAT THE SPIRIT OF HOMOSEXUALITY

I HAVE SPOKEN to you clearly in My Word that your body is not meant for immorality—it is meant to be for Me, and I want to fill your body with Myself. Don't you realize that your body is actually part of the body of Christ? Yet today you have allowed the vile spirit of homosexuality to dwell in your midst. It has corrupted and destroyed the lives of many, and you must repent, turn from all sexual sin, and commit your life to Me in holiness. Haven't you yet learned that your body is the home of the Holy Spirit I gave to you and that I live within you? Your own body does not belong to you, My daughter. I bought it with the great price of My Son's own death. So use every part of your body to give glory back to Me, because I own it.

1 CORINTHIANS 6

Prayer Declaration

Father, this nation has fallen prey to the wicked spirit of sexual immorality and homosexuality, and our nation is filled with people who not longer live in purity. Cause Your daughters to make a stand for purity. Lord, lead Your people to lead this nation to repent for its immorality and to turn to You in purity and dedication.

I WILL BRING NEW LIFE TO YOUR MORAL CONSCIENCE

MY DAUGHTER, IN the last days in which you live many have abandoned the faith and are following deceiving spirits and things taught by demons. Such teachings come through hypocritical liars, whose consciences have been seared as with a hot iron. I am calling you to return to righteousness and morality. The death and resurrection of My Son have saved you from the wickedness of a sinful lifestyle. Return to the shelter of My great love for you. Love Me with all of your heart, for love springs forth from a pure heart, a good conscience and a sincere faith. Make sure that you are living with a clear conscience and that you desire to live honorably in every way.

1 TIMOTHY 4:2; 1:5; HEBREWS 13:18

Prayer Declaration

Father, like the men who stood ready to stone the woman caught in the act of adultery, but who were convicted by their conscience and went out one by one, leaving Jesus alone to minister repentance to the woman, convict me of the sins I try to hide and fail to admit, and bring me to repentance.

I Will Fill You With Remorse for Your Sin

My daughter, consider your ways and search your heart to root out the wickedness and sin that have entered because of disobedience. Turn to Me with remorse for your disobedience, and turn from your sin. Do not practice the sins of this world. Do not despise the riches of My goodness, forbearance, and long-suffering, for they will lead you to repentance. Godly sorrow will produce repentance and will lead you to salvation, but the sins of this world will only produce death. Allow remorse to clean your hearts and remove the sinfulness from your life. I will be long-suffering toward you, for I am not willing that any should perish, but that you should come to repentance.

Romans 2:2–4; 2 Corinthians 7:10; 2 Peter 2:9

Prayer Declaration

Lord, I know that the works of the flesh are adultery, fornication, uncleanness, lewdness, idolatry, sorcery, hatred, contentions, jealousies, outbursts of wrath, selfish ambitions, dissensions, and heresies. Teach me to live by the power of Your Spirit and to destroy the works of the flesh out of my life. Give me remorse for my sins, and lead me to repentance.

I Will Make the "Acceptable" Unacceptable

The evil spirit of Belial has seared the conscience of many of My daughters and has caused them to accept the unacceptable as acceptable lifestyles. Do not allow your mind and conscience to be corrupted and to reject the truth in favor of impurity. I am grieved by your adulterous hearts, which have turned away from Me, and by your eyes, which have lusted after the idols of this world. I loathe your evil and all your detestable practices. Those who trust in worldly idols, who make the things of this world their gods, will be turned back in utter shame. I love you, My daughter. You are precious and honored in My sight, and I gave My own Son in exchange for your life. Do not be afraid, but turn back to Me and begin to live in purity once again.

Titus 1:15; Ezekiel 6:9; Isaiah 42:17; 43:4–5

Prayer Declaration

Lord, make me worthy of saying, as Paul did, that my conscience testifies that I have conducted myself in the world, and especially in my relationship with others, in the holiness and sincerity that come from You. I renounce secret and shameful ways. I will no longer accept the idols of this world, but I have rejected all sin and have turned in full surrender and commitment to You.

I WILL REMOVE DEFILEMENT FROM YOUR NATION

Do NOT DEFILE yourself with the wickedness that has defiled the nations of this world. For the nation that is defiled will suffer the punishment of its iniquities. Therefore keep My statues and My judgments, and do not commit the abominations of defilement. For I brought your nation like a vine out of captivity and planted it and prepared room for it. I caused it to take deep root and My righteousness to fill the land. Why have you allowed its hedges to be broken down that its fruit may be plucked by all who pass by the way? Return to Me, and I will visit your nation once again and will cause it to be fruitful and to multiply in My righteousness.

LEVITICUS 18:24; PSALM 80:8–15

Prayer Declaration

Father, restore our nation once again to righteousness, and remove defilement from our land. Let Your hand be upon us, and make us strong for Yourself. Revive us, and we will call upon Your name. Cause righteousness and praise to spring forth from this nation before all the nations.

I HAVE SHOWN YOU THE DANGERS
OF ALCOHOL

Do NOT BE beguiled by the pleasures of alcohol and by the pervasiveness of those who promote it. The spirit of Belial can operate through alcohol, leading many into drunkenness. Heed My Word, for who has woe? Who has sorrow? Who has strife? Who has complaints? Who has needless bruises? Who has bloodshot eyes? Those who linger over wine, who go to sample bowls of mixed wine. Do not gaze at wine when it is red, when it sparkles in the cup, when it goes down smoothly. In the end it bites like a snake and poisons like a viper. Your eyes will see strange sights, and your mind will imagine confusing things, and your heart will utter perverse things. My daughter, beware of the dangers of Belial who works through alcohol and drunkenness.

PROVERBS 23:29–35, NIV

Prayer Declaration

Father, help me to listen to the warning in Your Word to "take heed to yourselves, lest your hearts be weighed down with carousing, drunkenness, and cares of this life." Keep me focused on living for You, so that I am not caught in the devil's snare to cause me to be unprepared when You come back for Your pure bride.

I Will Reveal How Alcohol Leads to Perversity

BE AWARE THAT the spirit of perversion is at work through drunkenness. If you walk in uprightness, you will fear Me and live in purity, but if you become perverse in your ways, you will despise Me and walk in uncleanness. Perversion has spread throughout the nations through the spirit that works through alcohol and drunkenness. Heed My warning, and remove yourself far from the spirit of perversion. Avoid the works of the flesh that lead to perversion, which include sexual immorality, impurity, drunkenness, and the like. Those who live like this will not inherit the kingdom of God. Those who belong to Me have crucified the flesh with its passions and desires. Since My Holy Spirit lives within you, live by My Spirit and keep in step with Him.

PROVERBS 14:2; GALATIANS 5:19–25

Prayer Declaration

Lord, I want to do only what You want me to do, for following my own desires will lead me astray. Keep me from drunkenness, wild parties, and other evil things. I don't want to live like that, Lord. I want to honor and serve You in everything I do.

I WILL PROTECT YOUR YOUNG WOMEN FROM DATE RAPE

MY DAUGHTER, THE spirit of Belial at work through alcohol can open the door for the spirit of rape, including the danger My young daughters face today through date rape. Keep My young daughters from these dangers. Teach them to stay away from the pleasures of the world, including the pleasures of alcohol. Teach them not to associate with sexually immoral people—people who claim to be My children but who are sexually immoral, greedy, an idolater or slanderer, a drunkard or swindler. Show them by your own example what it means to be filled with My Spirit, speaking to one another with psalms, hymns, and songs from My Spirit.

1 CORINTHIANS 5:9–11; EPHESIANS 5:19–20

Prayer Declaration

Father, protect our young women from the dangers of date rape that often comes as a result of the pleasures of alcohol and debauchery. Help me to teach the young women to be careful about the kind of people they hang around. Teach them not to even associate with those who are controlled by the spirit of Belial. Help them to choose their friends wisely and to commit to live their lives in purity before You.

I Will Restore Your Youth to Purity

I have counseled you in My Word to love Me with all
your heart and with all your soul and with all your strength.
Impress My Word upon your children. Talk about it when
you sit at home and when you walk along the road, when you
lie down and when you get up. Let the little children come
to Me, and do not hinder them, for the kingdom of heaven
belongs to them. Do not exasperate your children, but bring
them up in the training and instruction of My ways. Do not
embitter your children, or they will become discouraged. In
this way you will restore the youth of your nation to Me and
will cause them to walk in purity and honor before Me.

Deuteronomy 6:5–9; Matthew 19:14;
Colossians 3:21

Prayer Declaration

*Father, let me be a part of Your great army of intercessors who
are calling the youth of this nation back to purity and cleanness
of heart. Bind the spirits of wickedness and sin from their evil
strategies to capture our youth, and loose the youth of this nation
from the stranglehold of sin. Let me stand in the gap and be a
watchman to prevent the destruction of our youth. Guard their
lives from immorality and idolatry, and raise up a mighty army
of youth who are passionate and pure in their walk before You.*

I Will Keep You From a Reprobate Mind

My Word warns you of the danger of refusing to acknowledge Me in your life, choosing instead to follow the passions of your own lust. Beware of becoming so estranged from Me that you have chosen to allow your mind to become depraved instead of retaining the knowledge of My ways. A reprobate mind will allow the enemy to fill your life with every kind of wickedness. The reprobate mind of sin is death, but if you allow your mind to be controlled by My Spirit, you will find peace and life. Do not conform any longer to the pattern of this world, but be transformed by the renewing of your mind. Then you will be able to test and approve what My will is—My good, pleasing, and perfect will.

Romans 1:28–32; 8:6; 12:2

Prayer Declaration

Father, teach me to protect my mind from the control of the enemy. I want only the knowledge of Your ways and will for my life. Protect Your daughters from the pull of the world that would cause them to be estranged from You. Help us to protect our minds from the subtle attack of the enemy and his desire to cause us to walk in wickedness. Let me live by Your good, pleasing, and perfect will for my life.

I Will Remove Lewdness From Your Land

You are living in the midst of a warped and crooked generation. The corrupt behaviors of this present generation have become a shame to those who seek to walk in My ways and to live just and upright lives. Do not follow the example of the host of disobedient people who act in lewd and vulgar manners. Remember the days when My people sought to walk in purity and wisdom and modesty before Me. Do not repay Me for My benefits with the foolishness and moral impurities of the world. Let My words descend like dew, like showers on new grass, like abundant rain on tender plants and water your heart with tenderness and moral purity.

DEUTERONOMY 32:1–7, NIV

Prayer Declaration

Father, Your Word tells me You are the rock; Your deeds are perfect. Everything You do is just and fair. You are a faithful God who does no wrong; how just and upright You are. But there are many people who have acted corruptly toward You with lewdness and perversity. They are a deceitful and twisted generation. Father, may everything I do show others that You are my rock. Cleanse me from all perverseness.

AUGUST 21

I WILL SET YOU FREE FROM PORNOGRAPHY

MY DAUGHTER, GUARD against the wickedness of the spirit of Belial that is flooding this present day with obscenities and sexual filth. Follow My instruction to have no part in that which is vile and perverse, and refuse to look upon that which is evil. Take a stand against the wicked who in their arrogance hunt down My little children who are weak and helpless and capture them so they pursue the evil cravings of their hearts. They lie in wait in the villages and ambush the innocent, just as a lion lies in wait to catch the helpless and drag them off in his net. Their victims are crushed and collapse and fall under his strength. I will set them free from the wicked and will punish the wicked with death. I will not forget the helpless or fail to see the trouble of the afflicted, for I will be a Father to the fatherless and call the evildoer to account for his wickedness.

PSALMS 101:3–4; 10:2, 8–15

Prayer Declaration

Father, I will sing of Your love and justice. I will be careful to lead a blameless life and to conduct the affairs of my house with a blameless heart. I will not look with approval on anything that is vile. I will have no part in it, and the perverse of heart will be far from me. I will have nothing to do with what is evil and will take a stand to loose the helpless captives of perversity from the stranglehold of the wicked.

I WILL REMOVE THE EVIL PLOTS OF LAWLESSNESS

BEWARE OF THOSE who plot against My righteousness and who devise wicked, lawless plans. Although they may have allies and are numerous, they will be destroyed and pass away. I will break their yoke from the necks of My daughters and will tear away the shackles of lawlessness from your land. Those who devise evil plots of lawlessness are a disgrace in My eyes. They practice deceit, and their words are like a sharpened razor. I will surely bring them down to everlasting ruin. I will uproot them from the land of the living. My righteous daughters will see My justice and will say, "Here now is the one who did not make God her stronghold but trusted in her great wealth and grew strong by destroying others!"

NAHUM 1:9–11; PSALM 52:1–7

Prayer Declaration

Father, just like David, I see the evil in our land, and I know that You will cause the plans of evildoers to fail. I will be still in Your presence and wait patiently for You to act. I will not worry about evil people who prosper, and I will not fret about their wicked schemes. I have committed my life to following Your instructions, Lord.

I WILL RESTORE YOUR JUDEO-CHRISTIAN FOUNDATION

WHEN WICKEDNESS REIGNS, the people do not know, neither do they understand, and they walk around in darkness. All the foundations are unstable when the wicked rule. My daughter, keep your eyes focused on My ways, and I will guide you continually. I will satisfy your soul in drought and strengthen your bones. You will be like a watered garden, like a spring of water whose waters do not fail. I will call those from among you who shall build the old waste places. You shall raise up the foundations of many generations. My people will be called the Repairers of the Breach, the Restorers of Streets to Dwell In.

PSALM 82:5; ISAIAH 58:11–12

Prayer Declaration

Father, in this day when it seems that godless men and godless laws are destroying the godly life and foundations on which this nation was founded, Your Word brings courage and strength to Your people. As we confidently trust in You to care for us, we will strengthen our hearts and do our part to once again raise up the Judeo-Christian foundations of many generations. Call us to be Repairers of the Breach and Restorers of Streets to Dwell In.

I Will Cast Out the Spirit of Rebellion

Do not be ignorant of the spirit of rebellion in the world today. My Word has told you that the kings of the earth rise up and the rulers band together against Me and against My anointed, saying, "Let us break their chains and throw off their shackles." This is the spirit of antichrist, and its ultimate goal is to cast off My restraint. The spirit of rebellion will lead many into disobedience. Remember the rebelliousness of the children of Israel. When they would not return to Me so that I could show them My grace and mercy, I would not let them enter the land of promise that I had given to them. But if My daughters will turn to Me from their rebelliousness, I will become their Father, and they will be My children. I will make the nations their inheritance and the ends of the earth their possession.

Psalm 2:2–3, 7–8

Prayer Declaration

Father, after the children of Israel had wandered in the wilderness for forty years, You confronted them about their rebelliousness and told them: "Understand that the Lord your God is not giving you this good land to possess because of your righteousness." Just as Moses pleaded with You to have mercy on the people and not destroy them, so I plead with You, Father, to forgive America for its rebelliousness and sin and to save our nation from destruction.

I Will Restore Restraint and Godliness

MY DAUGHTER, WHERE there is not vision, no redemptive revelation of My ways, the people cast off restraint. The people conspire against Me and follow the evil plots of wicked counselors. But although they are many and believe themselves to be safe, yet they will be cut down when I pass through. Because they refuse to recognize My revelation and My ways, I will no longer recognize their children. But if you will return to Me against whom you have revolted and reject the godlessness of this world, I will shield you and deliver you. I will forgive your rebellion and restore godliness to your land.

PROVERBS 29:18; HOSEA 4:4–10; ISAIAH 31:6–7

Prayer Declaration

Lord, Your Word has clearly identified the reason America is falling into godlessness and immorality. You tell us clearly, "Where there is no revelation (no vision [no redemptive revelation of God]), the people cast off restraint." This nation has forsaken the restraints of Your Word for their own godless, liberal agendas. Have mercy on America, Lord, and reestablish us in Your laws.

I Desire to Raise Up a Bold, Spiritual Army

My daughter, I have equipped you with weapons of warfare that will overcome the fleshly plots of wickedness and rebellion that have crept into the land. My weapons are mighty for pulling down strongholds and casting down arguments and every high thing that exalts itself against the knowledge of My ways. They are powerful enough to bring every thought into captivity to obedience, and they will be used to punish all disobedience. Do not fear the enemy! Rise up and speak My Word with boldness. My Holy Spirit is with you and will empower you to be successful.

2 Corinthians 10:3–6; Acts 4:29

Prayer Declaration

Lord, make us into a strong, bold spiritual army in America. We are human, but we don't wage war as humans do. We use Your mighty weapons, not worldly weapons, to knock down the strongholds of human reasoning and to destroy false arguments. We destroy every proud obstacle that keeps people from knowing You. We capture their rebellious thoughts and teach them to obey You. Move by Your Holy Spirit through us to destroy the influence of those who claim to know more than You do.

THE PLANS OF EVILDOERS WILL FAIL

I TAKE NO pleasure in the wickedness of man and will not allow evil to dwell among My people. The boastful will not stand in My sight, nor will the way of the workers of iniquity prosper. I will destroy those who speak falsehood, for I abhor bloodthirsty and deceitful men. My daughter, I have instructed My people to depart from evil and to do good. I have counseled you not to fret because of evildoers, nor to be envious of the workers of iniquity. For I will cause their evil plans to fail. They will soon be cut down like the grass and wither as the green herb. Trust in Me, do good, and dwell in the land. Delight yourself in My ways, and I will give you the desires of your heart.

PSALMS 5:4–6; 37:1–4

Prayer Declaration

Father, I see the evil in our land, and I know that You will cause the plans of evildoers to fail. I will obey Your Word to turn from evil and do good, for You love justice, and You will never abandon the godly. I have committed my life to following Your instructions, Lord.

I WILL FILL YOUR LAND WITH
GODLY LAWMAKERS

I AM GRACIOUS and full of compassion and righteousness. I will bless the man who delights greatly in My ways. I will raise up those who are willing to lead My people in righteousness. I will establish My principles in the laws of your land and will honor those who uphold them. A good woman deals graciously and lends. She will guide her affairs with discretion. She will not be shaken or fearful of evil tidings, for her heart is steadfast because she trusts in Me. She has dispersed abroad and has given to the poor. She will be exalted with honor, and she will guide My people in integrity and establish My foundation of righteousness in the land.

PSALM 112

Prayer Declaration

Father, sometimes unjust leaders boldly claim God is on their side, yet they permit injustice. They gang up on the righteous and condemn the innocent to death through their unjust laws and regulations. But when this happens, You are my fortress and the mighty rock on which I stand. You have promised to turn their sins back upon them and destroy them in the way they planned to destroy Your children. Raise up a nation governed in righteousness. Place godly leaders in place who will create laws based on Your principles.

I WILL RESCUE YOU FROM EVIL PEOPLE

I WILL DELIVER you from evil men and will preserve you from violent men who plan evil things in their hearts. They have purposed to make your steps stumble. The proud have laid a snare for you, but I will cover your head in the day of battle. I will not grant the desires of the wicked or further their evil schemes. I will maintain the cause of the afflicted and justice for the poor. The righteous will give thanks to My name, and the upright will dwell in My presence. No grave trouble will overtake My righteous daughters, but the wicked will be filled with evil.

PSALM 140; PROVERBS 12:21

Prayer Declaration

Father, You have promised that whoever listens to You will dwell safely and will be secure, without fear of evil. Keep me out of the hands of the wicked. Do not let evil people have their way. Do not let their evil schemes succeed. I will help those who are persecuted by evildoers and will give justice to the poor. Surely righteous people will praise Your name, and the godly will live in Your presence.

I WILL PREVENT INJUSTICE AND INEQUITY

MY DAUGHTER, I will loose the chains of injustice and untie
the cords of the yoke to set free those oppressed by inequity. I
will thwart the plans of the crafty so that their hands achieve
no success. I will catch the wise in their craftiness, and the
schemes of the wily will be swept away. I will save the needy
from the sword in their mouth and will save them from the
clutches of the powerful.

JOB 5:12–16; JEREMIAH 22:16; ISAIAH 58:11

Prayer Declaration

*Lord, You love righteousness and justice and will foil the plans of
the nations and thwart the purposes of the unjust. We wait in hope
for You to act. You are our help and our shield, and in You our
hearts rejoice, for we trust in Your holy name. May Your unfailing
love rest upon us, O Lord, even as we put our hope in You.*

BUILD YOUR LIFE ON RIGHTEOUSNESS

WOE TO HER who builds her mansion by unrighteousness and injustice and makes her countrymen work for nothing, not paying them for their labor. I will defend the cause of the poor and needy. If you do away with the yoke of oppression and spend yourself on behalf of the hungry, satisfying the needs of the oppressed, then your light will rise in the darkness and your night will become like the noonday. I will guide you always and satisfy your needs and strengthen your frame.

LUKE 1:75; ACTS 10:35; ROMANS 6:13–14

Prayer Declaration

Lord, You have delivered us from the hands of our enemies that we might live before You in holiness and righteousness. Cause this to be a nation that fears You and produces works of righteousness, that we might be accepted by You. Sin will not have dominion over us, but we will become instruments of Your righteousness all the days of our lives.

SEPTEMBER

Activating the Blessing of God

My Favor Is My Gift to You

My daughter, I bestow My favor on those who follow after My ways. Because of the gift of My favor, I released My children from their captivity in Egypt and did not send them away empty-handed. They left with the plunder of the Egyptians. When Gideon asked Me for a sign of My favor, I caused My fire to consume his sacrifice to Me. I will bless My righteous servants and will surround them and protect them as with a shield. Follow after Me in all your ways, for whoever finds Me finds life and obtains My favor. Serve Me with the righteousness of Your heart, turn to Me in all your ways, and you will find My favor. I will bless your life and will protect you and guide you in all your ways.

Genesis 33:8; 47:29; Psalm 5:12; Proverbs 8:35

Prayer Declaration

Lead me, O Lord, in Your righteousness; make my way straight before Your face, and I will come into Your house in the multitude of Your mercy. Bestow Your gift of favor upon my life, for I put my trust in You. I will be joyful in You, and You will surround me with Your favor as with a shield.

MY FAVOR BREAKS YOUR CAPTIVITY

IF YOU TURN to Me with all your heart and serve Me in My ways, I will break your captivity and will loose the bondage of Satan from your life. I will be merciful to you and will raise you up and will repay your enemies for their treatment toward you. You will know that I am well pleased with you because your enemies will not triumph over you. I will uphold you in your integrity and will set you before My face forever. My favor will be new every morning to you, like the dew upon the grass. In My presence you will find the light of My face, and My favor will be like a cloud of the latter rain upon you.

PSALMS 85:1; 41:10–12; PROVERBS 16:15

Prayer Declaration

*Father, I praise You for breaking the captivity of my enemies
and for loosing me from the bonds of wickedness. Your name
will endure forever, and Your name will be remembered for all
generations. For You will arise and have favor upon me, for the
set time of my favor has come. You will not disregard my prayer
in my destitution or despise it. I will praise You as long as I
live, and my children shall be established in favor before you.*

MY FAVOR IS BETTER THAN RICHES

DAUGHTER, A GOOD name is to be chosen rather than great riches, and My loving favor is better than silver or gold. By humility and holy fear you will receive My riches and honor and life. I will be the glory of your strength, and My favor will be a shield of protection for you. I will grant you life and favor, and My care will preserve your spirit. In My favor I will have mercy upon you and will keep your gates of sustenance and prosperity open continually. I will cause the wealth of the nations to flow into your gates, and the glory of prosperity will fall upon you. I will give you favor in the presence of the kings and rulers of this world, and will give you a position of honor, and will cause your life to overflow with My sustenance.

PROVERBS 22:1; ISAIAH 60:10–13; ACTS 7:10–11

Prayer Declaration

*I will extol You, O Lord, for You have lifted me up and brought
my soul up from the grave. Although my weeping may endure for a night, Your joy comes in the morning. You have
turned for me my mourning into dancing. You have put off
my sackcloth and clothed me with gladness. I will sing praise
to You and not be silent; I will give thanks to You forever.*

I WILL SHOW YOU MY LOVING-KINDNESS

I WILL SHOW My marvelous loving-kindness to those who put their trust in Me. I will keep you as the apple of My eye and hide you under the shadow of My wings. I will satisfy you with the abundance of My house and will give you drink from My river of delights. In Me is the fountain of life, and in My light is the light for your path. I will not take My love from you, nor will I ever betray My faithfulness. I will forgive all your iniquities and heal all your diseases. I will redeem your life from destruction and crown you with loving-kindness and tender mercies. I am merciful and gracious, slow to anger, and abounding in mercy. I will revive you according to My loving-kindness.

PSALMS 17:7; 89:33; 103:4, 8

Prayer Declaration

Father, hear my voice according to Your loving-kindness. Revive me according to Your justice. Plead my cause and redeem me; revive me according to Your Word. Great are Your tender mercies, O Lord; revive me according to Your loving-kindness. The entirety of Your Word is truth, and every one of Your righteous judgments endures forever. I rejoice at Your Word as one who finds great treasure.

THE BLESSING OF JABEZ

REMEMBER MY SERVANT Jabez, who called upon Me, saying, "Oh, that You would bless me indeed, and enlarge my territory, that Your hand would be with me, and that You would keep me from evil, that I may not cause pain!" I granted him what he had requested, just as I do with My daughters today. I enlarged the inheritance of Gad because he administered My justice and judgments with the people of Israel. I allowed Isaac to sow in the land of Abimelech, king of the Philistines, and prospered him to reap a hundredfold in one year and enabled him to become so prosperous that the Philistines envied him. I will enlarge your territory, My child, and will bless your life with the abundance of My inheritance for you.

1 CHRONICLES 4:10, NKJV; DEUTERONOMY 33:21;
GENESIS 26:12–14

Prayer Declaration

Father, thank You for blessing my substance and the work of my hands. Enlarge me like Gad, and bless my life as You blessed the lives of Isaac and Jabez. Let me dwell in safety under Your protection and covering as You covered Your children in the Bible. Bless my beginning and my latter end as You did with Job. I will praise You for Your abundant blessings and honor You with my life.

Daughter, I Will Not Let You Go

When Jacob repented of his sin against his brother, he sought his brother's forgiveness and sent an offering of his abundance as an act of reconciliation. Then he returned to the land where Esau dwelt to establish a relationship of trust with him once again. When he stepped onto his brother's land, I appeared to him and wrestled with him through the night. When the day was breaking and I made ready to leave his presence, Jacob cried out to Me and said, "I will not let You go unless You bless me!" Because he had prevailed in his struggle with Esau, and because he prevailed in his struggle with Me, I blessed him there and preserved his life. My daughter, do not give up in your determination to seek My blessing. Seek My face, just as Jacob did, and I will preserve your life.

Genesis 32

Prayer Declaration

Father, teach me to hold on to the promises You have given to me, even when I have to contend for them in a battle with the supernatural. Help me to remember that You possess all the provisions I need and that You have asked me to come to You and request Your blessing upon my life. Let me meet with You face-to-face, and bless me with a new name, a new purpose, a new future, and new destiny. Truly You love to give good gifts to Your daughters.

I WILL SHOW YOU MY GLORY

MOSES LONGED TO see My glory and to dwell in My shadow. He sought hard after Me, and I knew him intimately. He found grace in My sight, and I knew him by name. My daughter, seek after Me intimately, so that I will know you by name. Ask to see My glory, just as Moses asked. I will cause My goodness to pass before you. My goodness includes the blessings of goods, good things, goodness, property, fairness, beauty, joy, and prosperity. I have an abundant store of goodness, and I am anxious to give good gifts to My children. My blessings are stored up for those who know Me and those whom I know. All you have to do is to ask Me to bless you.

EXODUS 33:17–23

Prayer Declaration

Lord, You are the source of my blessing. I choose Your blessings by walking in Your covenant. I will knock on the door of blessing, and You will open it to me. You are a God who blesses and rewards those who diligently seek after You. Rain upon my life, and pour out Your blessing over me.

I WILL BE A FOUNTAIN OF LIFE TO YOU

I AM THE fountain of life, and I will allow you to drink freely from the river of My pleasures. My faithfulness to you reaches from the heavens, and My righteousness is like the great mountains. Therefore put your trust under the shadow of My wings, and I will abundantly satisfy you with the fullness of My house. My words will be life to your soul and grace to your life. Hold fast to My instruction, and seek after My wisdom, for in them you will find life and obtain My favor. I will show you the path of life, and you will dwell in My presence in fullness of joy. At My right hand you will find pleasures forevermore.

PSALMS 36:5–9; 16:11

Prayer Declaration

Lord, You are my fountain of life, and Your wisdom will be like a tree of life to me. Your words are life to my soul and grace to my body. I will hold fast to Your instruction, because it is my life. I will seek after Your wisdom, for in it I will find life and obtain Your favor. I will praise You for Your goodness and Your wonderful works toward me.

I HAVE GIVEN YOU THE BLESSING OF ABRAHAM

DAUGHTER, COME TO ME with a faithful spirit. When I ask you to be willing to give Me those things that are most precious to you, just as I asked Abraham to sacrifice his only son, follow the example of Abraham and respond willingly and obediently. Then I will give you the blessing of Abraham. I will bless you and will multiply your descendants as the stars of the heaven and as the sand, which is on the seashore. Your descendants will possess the gate of their enemies. Your seed will become a blessing to all the nations of the earth because you have obeyed My voice.

GENESIS 22:1–19

Prayer Declaration

Let Your blessing come upon my family. I am blessed through Christ, the seed of Abraham. Bless me greatly, just as You blessed Abraham. Let those connected to me be blessed, and may my descendants serve You fully and shine Your light to all the nations of the world.

I WILL BLESS THE WORK OF YOUR HANDS

I AM A God of provision, and I love to bless My daughters who serve Me out of the faithfulness of their hearts. I will bless your substance and accept the work of your hands. Honor Me with your work, and remember the needs of the stranger, the fatherless, and the widow that I will be able to bless you in all the work of your hands. Be strong, and do not let your hands be weak, for your work will be rewarded. Like My servant Nehemiah, set your hands to do the good work that I have placed in your heart, for I Myself will prosper you. Speak boldly of My goodness, confirming the message of My grace from My Word, and I will enable you to do miraculous signs and wonders in My name.

DEUTERONOMY 33:11; 24:19–21; NEHEMIAH 2:18;

ACTS 14:3

Prayer Declaration

Lord, bless my substance and the work of my hands. Give me favor like Nehemiah to finish the assignment You have given me. I will serve You with gladness, for it is You who has made us and established us, and not we ourselves. I will enter Your gates with thanksgiving and come into Your courts with praise, for You are good, Your mercy is everlasting, and Your truth will endure to all generations.

ACTIVATING THE BLESSING OF GOD

I WILL BLESS YOU WITH WISDOM LIKE SOLOMON

DO NOT SEEK the wisdom of mankind or think that man's understanding will bring you long life. To Me alone belong wisdom and power; counsel and understanding are Mine. Man cannot comprehend the worth of My wisdom, nor can it be purchased with silver and gold. It cannot be compared with fine jewels, nor can it be found by searching for it. I alone understand the way to wisdom and where it dwells. But if you desire it with all your heart and will come to Me and ask Me for My wisdom, as My servant Solomon did, I will give it to you, My daughter. Make My wisdom the desire of your heart, and I will grant to you what you have asked.

JOB 28:12–21; 2 CHRONICLES 1:7–12

Prayer Declaration

Lord, bless me with wisdom as You did Solomon. I desire truth in my heart, and You will teach me wisdom in the inmost place. Your wisdom will give me discipline and insight, that I may do what is right and just and fair. Wisdom will save me from the ways of wickedness and keep me on the path of the righteous. There is no wisdom, no insight, no plan that can succeed against You. Let the Spirit of wisdom and understanding rest on me, and I will delight myself in You.

I Will Fulfill My Promise of Goodness

BECAUSE I WAS pleased with My servant Moses and knew him by name, I caused My goodness to pass in front of him, assuring him that I am compassionate and gracious, slow to anger, abounding in love and faithfulness, maintaining love to thousands, and forgiving wickedness, rebellion, and sin. Just as I fulfilled My promise of goodness to Moses, so too will I fulfill My promise of goodness to you, My daughter. Great in the presence of men is the goodness that I have laid up for those who fear and trust Me. I will hide you in the secret place of My presence, far from the plots of man. I will keep you secretly in a pavilion from the strife of many tongues. I will preserve you for your faithfulness. So be of good courage, for I will strengthen your heart because you have placed your hope in Me.

EXODUS 34:6–7; PSALM 31:19–20, 23–24

Prayer Declaration

Father, You have met me with the blessings of Your goodness and set a crown of righteousness upon my head. I asked You for life, and You gave it to me, length of days forever and ever. You have placed honor and majesty upon me and have made me exceedingly glad in Your presence. Let goodness and mercy follow me all the days of my life, for You are my shepherd, and I will not want.

I WILL ESTABLISH GOODNESS AND PROSPERITY IN YOUR LIFE

MY DAUGHTER, CALL to Me, and I will answer you and show you great and mighty things, which you do not know. I will cleanse you from all your iniquity against Me, and I will pardon all your iniquities and transgressions. Your name will be a name of joy, a praise and honor before all nations of the earth who hear of the good that I do to you. They will fear and tremble for all the goodness and all the prosperity that I provide to you. I will bring you into a plentiful country where you will enjoy My goodness. I will redeem you and ransom you from the hand of one stronger than you. Your enemies will see the stream of My goodness to you—the wheat and new wine and oil for your flocks. Your soul will be like a well-watered garden, and you will sorrow no more.

JEREMIAH 33:3, 8–9; 2:7; 31:11–12

Prayer Declaration

Lord, You have laid up Your great goodness for me; it will continually be in my life. Let me be satisfied with the goodness of Your house. Fill my soul with Your goodness, and establish goodness and prosperity in my life. I will praise You for your loving-kindness and great goodness to me.

I WILL SHOW YOU THE PATH OF LIFE

I WILL SHOW you the path of life, and in My presence I will give you fullness of joy. I will broaden the path beneath you and teach you My way. Take confidence in this: you will see My goodness in the land of the living. Wait for Me to move; be strong and take heart and wait for Me. My Word will be a lamp to your feet and a light for your path. I will make the path of the righteous level and smooth. I will make a way through the sea and a path through the mighty waters. Forget the former things; do not dwell on the past. See, I am doing a new thing! I am making a way in the desert for you, and streams in the wasteland.

PSALMS 16:11; 18:36; ISAIAH 43:16, 18–21

Prayer Declaration

Lord, show me the path of life; in Your presence is fullness of joy, and at Your right hand are pleasures forevermore. I will bless You because You have given me counsel and have instructed me in the night seasons. I have set You always before me, and I shall not be moved. Your Word is a lamp to my feet and a light to My path.

I HAVE REDEEMED YOUR LIFE
FROM DESTRUCTION

My DAUGHTER, BLESS Me with all that is within you, and forget not all My benefits to you. I have forgiven all your iniquities and healed all your diseases. I have redeemed your life from destruction and crowned you with loving-kindness and tender mercies. I will satisfy your mouth with good things and renew your youth like the eagle's. As high as the heavens are above the earth, so great is My mercy toward you. I will answer you when you call with awesome deeds of righteousness and will establish you with My strength as I established the mountain. I will clothe you with power and crown your year with goodness. The paths on which you walk will drip with abundance, and the pastures will be clothed with flocks and the valleys covered with grain.

PSALM 103:1–5

Prayer Declaration

Lord, I receive Your blessing, for my transgression is forgiven and my sin is covered. You have blessed me and chosen me and caused me to approach You and dwell in Your courts that I might be satisfied with the goodness of Your house. I will dwell in Your house forever and will continue to praise Your name. I will fear Your name and delight greatly in all Your commandments.

YOU WILL DWELL IN MY HOUSE FOREVER

THE STEPS OF a good woman are ordered by Me, and I delight in her way. Depart from evil, and do good that you may dwell with Me forevermore. For I am a God who loves justice and does not forsake My daughters. They are preserved forever. My righteous will inherit My land and will dwell in it forever. Let not your heart be troubled, for in My Father's house are many mansions. I will prepare a place for you and will come again and receive you to Myself, that where I am, there you may be also. Let not your heart be troubled or afraid, for you have heard Me say to you that I am going away, but I am coming back to you. Goodness and mercy will follow you all the days of your life, and you will dwell in My house forever.

PSALM 37:23–24, 29; JOHN 14:27–28; PSALM 23:6

Prayer Declaration

Lord, bless me as I dwell in Your house and continue to praise you. I trust in You, and my hope is in You. Prepare a place in Your presence where I can dwell forever. I will not be troubled or afraid, for I know that You will come back for Me and will take Me with You to live forever in your eternal home.

My Correction Will Be a Blessing to You

Do not despise My chastening or detest My correction. For those whom I love, I correct, just as a father the daughter in whom he delights. I know that no chastening and correction seems joyous when you receive it, but grievous. Nevertheless, afterward it can yield the fruit of righteousness in all who are exercised thereby. Therefore make straight the paths for your feet, lest you be turned out of the way. Accept My correction, for it will bring healing to your life. Follow My peace and holiness, and look diligently unto your ways, lest any root of bitterness springs up to trouble you and cause you to be defiled. Those who refuse to receive My correction and make their faces hard will not know My ways or blessings.

Hebrews 12:7–15; Jeremiah 5:3

Prayer Declaration

Father, let me be blessed by Your correction, and teach me out of Your Word, for I fear Your name and delight greatly in Your commandments. I will accept correction through Your Word, for Your Word is God-breathed and is useful for teaching, rebuking, correcting, and training me in righteousness, so that I may be thoroughly equipped for every good work.

PLACE YOUR HOPE IN ME

TRUST IN ME in all your ways, for your hope lies only in Me. Give Me your love for I will preserve the faithful. Be of good courage, daughter, and strengthen your heart. My eye is on those who fear Me and who hope in My mercy. I will deliver your soul from death and keep you alive in distress. Wait for Me, for I am your help and your shield. Rejoice in Me and trust My name, for I will reward your hope. Wait for Me like those who watch for the morning, for with Me you will find mercy and abundant redemption from all your iniquities. Rejoice in the hope of My glory, knowing that tribulation produces perseverance, and perseverance, character, and character, hope. Hope will not disappoint you, because I have poured out in your hearts the Holy Spirit.

PSALMS 31:23–24; 33:18–22; 130:6–8

Prayer Declaration

Bless me, Lord. I trust in You, and my hope is in You. I will be fervent in spirit as I serve only You. I will rejoice in hope, be patient in tribulation, and continue steadfastly in prayer. May Your hope fill me with all joy and peace in believing, that I may abound in hope by the power of the Holy Spirit.

YOUR OBEDIENCE BRINGS MY BLESSINGS

IN MY WORD I have laid out My plan for how My children can receive My blessing. Be careful to do all that I have commanded, and My blessing will flow out to you and to your children, your cattle, and your servants. Everything your hand touches or foot treads upon will be successful. Obedience will also bring you the blessing of protection from your enemies, for I will be your strong tower. If you obey Me, My daughter, I will bless you with life and will release you from death. My Son died on the cross to release you from death. All you have to do to receive My gift is to walk in My way by being obedient to My Word.

DEUTERONOMY 11

Prayer Declaration

Lord, I pray that You will have confidence in my obedience, for I will put myself to the test to be obedient in all things. May all the blessings of the Lord come upon me and overtake me, because I obey Your voice. You will not cast me away, because I will be obedient to You. I will walk after Your ways and obey You in all things. I will serve You and hold fast to You.

Your Obedience Activates Your Faith

My daughter, the way that I will know you love Me is by your love to Me and your obedience to My instructions. My commandments are not burdensome, for through your obedience you will overcome the world. It is your faith that overcomes the world. What good is your faith, if it is not accompanied by your actions? Without action, faith is dead. Your obedience demonstrates to Me that you trust Me and believe I know what is best for you and that you are honoring your commitment to follow Me. If you want to receive My blessings, you must demonstrate that I am the Lord of your life. Your obedience in the testing ground will do that. Trust Me with all your plans, love Me by keeping My Word, do not sin against Me, and I will shower My blessings down upon you.

1 John 5:2–3; James 2:17; Luke 10:27

Prayer Declaration

Father, I am willing and obedient to Your will. I present myself to obey You, Lord; therefore I am a slave of obedience leading to righteousness. I thank You that You made me righteous through Your obedience. I will not obey unrighteousness; I will obey Your truth. I will receive Your blessing because I obey Your commandments.

By Obedience You Will Enter My Rest

It was because of their disobedience that the Israelites whom Moses led out of the wilderness did not enter into My rest. I was grieved with that generation because they always erred in their hearts and did not know My ways, so I would not allow them to enter into My rest. Take heed, My daughter, and do not depart from My way, for if you do, your unbelief will keep you from entering into My place of eternal rest. Nothing is hidden from My sight, but everything is uncovered and laid bare before My eyes. Therefore hold firmly to the faith you profess. Approach My throne with confidence in your obedient actions, and you will receive My mercy and find grace to help you. You will indeed enter into My rest.

Hebrews 4

Prayer Declaration

Let me not be like those who would not walk in Your ways and were not obedient to Your laws. I present myself to obey You, Lord, and I will cast down anything that exalts itself against Your knowledge, bringing all my thoughts captive to my determination to follow the obedience of Christ. I will obey You so that I may enter into Your rest. I will receive Your blessings, because I obey all Your ways.

I Will Incline My Ear Unto You

When I brought My people out of the land of Egypt, I commanded them to walk in all My ways that it might be well with them. Yet they did not obey or incline their ear to Me, but they followed the counsels and the dictates of their evil hearts and went backward and not forward. They stiffened their necks against My ways. Therefore because they did not obey My voice or receive correction, I rejected them and did not let them enter the land of promise.

Jeremiah 7:21–31

Prayer Declaration

I will obey Your Word, O Lord, and will incline my ear to Your voice. I will not follow the counsels and dictates of my evil heart. I will walk in all the ways You have commanded me, that it may be well with me. I will amend my ways and my doings according to Your Word. Let no one bewitch me that I should not obey the truth.

I WILL NOT LET SIN REIGN

MY DAUGHTER, DO not continue in sin once you have accepted the free gift of salvation offered by the death and resurrection of My Son. He died for your sins that you would no longer need to live in sin. Your old man of sin was crucified with Him, that your body of sin might be done away with—crucified—and you are no longer enslaved to sin. Do not let sin reign in your mortal body. You have been raised in new life from the dead, and you have become an instrument of righteousness to Me. My grace has set you free from sin. Begin to produce the fruit of holiness and righteousness, for My gift to you is eternal life in Christ Jesus.

GALATIANS 6

Prayer Declaration

I will not let sin reign in my mortal body, nor will I obey its lusts. Never again will I be bound, for Christ has made me free. I am free indeed! I will produce the fruit of righteousness and holiness. Never again will I walk in the works of the flesh, but I will manifest the fruit of the Spirit.

I Will Cause You to Walk in My Ways

I DESIRE ABOVE all things that you would obey My voice and walk in My ways. Come and draw near to Me, and I will teach you My ways. I will light your path that you can walk in My light. Blessed are the undefiled who walk in My Word and keep My testimonies. If you will seek Me with your whole heart and do no iniquity, you will be blessed. Daughter, walk as a child of light, finding out what is acceptable to Me. Have no fellowship with the unfruitful works of darkness, but rather expose them. Walk circumspectly, not foolishly, but as one who is wise, redeeming the time, because you are living in a time of evil. Walk in wisdom toward those who do not know Me. Let your speech always be with grace, seasoned with salt, that you may know how you ought to answer each person.

JEREMIAH 7:23; ISAIAH 2:3; EPHESIANS 5:8, 15;
COLOSSIANS 4:5

Prayer Declaration

Teach me Your way, O Lord, and I will walk in Your truth. Give me an undivided heart that I may fear Your name. I will praise You, O Lord, my God, with all my heart. For great is Your love toward me. You have delivered me from the depths of the grave. Show me the way that I should go, for to You I lift up my soul. Teach me to do your will, for You are my God.

YOUR FEAR OF THE LORD WILL BE YOUR FOUNDATION

TRUST IN ME, and I will be your helper and shield. Fear My name, and I will bless you. I will give you increase more and more, you and your children. Your fear of the Lord is pure and will endure forever. My ordinances are sure and altogether righteous. They are more precious than gold, than much pure gold. They are sweeter than honey from the honeycomb. By them I will give you warning to guide your life, and in keeping My words will be great reward. The fear of the Lord will teach you wisdom and humility, which will come with honor. It leads to life, and you will rest content, untouched by trouble. Your fear of the Lord will be the sure foundation for your times, a rich store of salvation and wisdom and knowledge.

PSALMS 115:11–14; 19:9–11; PROVERBS 19:23;
ISAIAH 33:6

Prayer Declaration

Father, I will fear the Lord and obey Your voice. I will walk in Your light and not in darkness. I place my trust and reliance only in You. My fear of You will be a secure fortress for me and a refuge for my children. It is a fountain of life and will turn me from the snares of death. I will walk in the way of righteousness along the paths of justice and favor from You.

I WILL BRING YOU INTO A LAND OF MILK AND HONEY

JUST AS I delivered the children of Israel out of the hand of the Egyptians and brought them up from that land to a land flowing with milk and honey, so I will deliver you. I have heard your cries and have seen the oppression of your enemies. The land I will give you is full of the hills and valleys of abundance that drink My rain from heaven. It is a land where I will care for you. I will give you the rain for your land in its season, the early rain and the latter rain, that you may gather in your grain, your new wine, and your oil. I will send grass in your fields for your livestock, that you may eat and be filled. Cross over into the land I am giving you; possess it and dwell in it.

DEUTERONOMY 11

Prayer Declaration

Bring me into a land flowing with milk and honey. Let me enjoy Your blessing like butter and honey, and let milk flow into my life from the hill of Zion. Bring me into a land filled with Your grain, which will cause me to grow spiritually. Let me receive the new wine of Your Spirit and the oil of Your anointing upon my life. Feed me with the finest of the wheat, and satisfy me with honey out of the rock of Your salvation.

ACTIVATING THE BLESSING OF GOD

UNDERSTAND THE BLESSING OF GIVING

MY DAUGHTER, KNOW this—it is more blessed to give than to receive. Give, and it will be given to you. A good measure, pressed down, shaken together, and running over, will be poured into your life. For with the measure you give, it will be given back to you. Freely you have received, freely give. Try Me now in this—if you give willingly to Me, see if I will not open for you the windows of heaven and pour out for you such blessing that there will not be room enough to receive it. I will rebuke the devourer for you so that he will not destroy the fruit of your ground, nor will the vine fail to bear fruit for you in the field. All nations will call you blessed, for you will be a delightful land.

LUKE 6:38; MATTHEW 10:8; MALACHI 3:10–12

Prayer Declaration

Truly it is more blessed to give than to receive. I will honor You with the firstfruits of my increase. I will bring my tithes and offerings to Your storehouse. Let the windows of heaven be opened over my life. I will sow into good ground, and You will enable me to reap an abundant harvest. Let my prayers and giving come up as a memorial before You. I will minister to You, Lord, with my substance.

YOU WILL BLOSSOM LIKE LEBANON

IF YOU WILL serve Me with all of your heart, I will cause you to blossom like the Valley of Lebanon. I will fill your life with the fragrance of beautiful flowers that you may draw many to My rest. I will cause you to be strong like the cedars of Lebanon, able to withstand the storms of life. Your life will provide shade for the weary travelers, comfort from the winds of tribulation, and strength against the attacks of the enemy. Your testimony will be an oasis from the wilderness of sin, and you will draw many to the living waters I will cause to flow into your life and out of it.

JOSHUA 11:17, PSALMS 72:16; 92:12, ISAIAH 35:2

Prayer Declaration

Father, I receive the majesty of Lebanon because I am in Your kingdom. Let me grow and be strong as the cedars of Lebanon. Let fruitfulness and abundance be upon my life. You created Lebanon for Your glory, and it is a symbol of the majesty of Your kingdom. Let the reality of Lebanon be released in my life. Let the river of God flow from Your holy mountain and water my land, and let me be an oasis of Your blessing to those who are weary.

YOU WILL NOT LACK ANY GOOD THING

DAUGHTER, IF YOU will seek My face, you shall not lack any good thing. My eyes are on the righteous, and My ears are open to their cry. I will deliver you out of all your troubles. I will be near to you when you have a broken heart, and I will save you when you come to me with a contrite spirit. Follow My Word spoken through My servant Paul to make it your ambition to lead a quiet life, to mind your own business, and to work with your hands, so that your daily life may win the respect of outsiders and so that you may lack nothing.

PSALM 34:10, 18; 1 THESSALONIANS 4:12

Prayer Declaration

Father, I will give of myself to You and to others, that I will not lack any good thing. I will serve you fully, so that You can supply me from the goodness of Your storehouse in heaven. I will honor You with the firstfruits of my increase, so that You can fill my barns with plenty. I will give, and give freely, so You can give to me—pressed down, shaken together, and running over.

I WILL OPEN THE WINDOWS OF HEAVEN

My DAUGHTER, GIVE of your substance to Me freely, that I might give to you. Test Me in this, for I will open up the windows of heaven for you and pour out a blessing so great you won't have room enough to take it in. If you serve Me faithfully with your life, I will pour water on your thirsty land and cause streams of blessing to flow on dry ground. I will pour out My Spirit on your offspring and My blessing on your descendants. My living water will flow from heaven into your life, and you will never thirst again.

MALACHI 3:10; ISAIAH 44:3

Prayer Declaration

Water my life, O Lord, and let Your living waters gush forth in every wilderness area of my life. Let my life become a fruitful field, and let me feed upon the abundance from heaven. I will give my life in faithfulness to You, and I will honor You in all I do.

OCTOBER

Rendering the
Enemy Helpless

HEALING IS AVAILABLE TO ALL

MY DAUGHTER, YOU do not have to be sick. My Son has taken the victory over death and illness from the enemy through His resurrection from the dead. He has made you alive together with Him, and He has forgiven all your trespasses and healed all your diseases. My Holy Spirit has filled your life with miraculous power, and in My name you have the authority to cast out demons, speak with new tongues, and lay hands on the sick and they recover. I have established My kingdom on earth, and in My presence and glory no sin or sickness can coexist. Establish My kingdom in your heart and life, and walk in healing and victory.

COLOSSIANS 2:12–13; MARK 16:17

Prayer Declaration

Father, thank You that through Your Son You have given me victory over death and illness. Thank You for making me alive with Christ. Through His gift on the cross He has forgiven all my sins and healed all my diseases. Fill me with Your Holy Spirit and with the power and authority to cast out demons, speak with new tongues, and lay hands on the sick and they recover.

PRESS FORWARD FOR YOUR HEALING

My daughter, expect your healing and press forward to Me
just as the woman with the issue of blood pressed forward to
touch the hem of My garment. Call to Me for help, and I will
heal you and bring you up from the grave. Press forward to
Me for your healing. Seek to understand My ways, and open
your eyes to My truth. Do not allow your ears to become dull
or your eyes to close. Understand with your heart, and turn to
Me and I will heal you. Do not become discouraged; put your
mind on Me. Don't let anyone stop you. Just as the woman
pressed forward, reached Me, and was healed by touching My
garment, you too can press, reach up, and grab your healing.

MATTHEW 9:20; PSALM 30:2–3; ISAIAH 6:9–10

Prayer Declaration

*Father, give me the determination to reach You and to touch
You for my healing that the woman with the issue of blood
had. Don't let my ears become dull to Your voice or my
eyes closed from seeking Your face. Like Paul, I will press
toward the mark for the prize of the high calling of God
in Christ Jesus. I will trust in You for my healing.*

CLOSE YOUR MIND TO THE ENEMY

LOOK WITH YOUR eyes and hear with your ears, and fix your mind on the truths of My Word. Close your mind to the discouraging and defeating distractions of the enemy. The mind of sinful man is death, but the mind that is controlled by My Spirit is filled with life and peace. Remember the example of Peter, who took his eyes off of Me and placed them on the dangers of the sea. The enemy tried to close his mind to what he could do through Me. Just so the enemy will try to close your mind to the victory and healing that can be yours through Me. The enemy wants to fill your mind with doubts, but I have instructed you to fix your thoughts on things that are true, noble, just, pure, lovely, and of good report. Meditate on these things, and trust Me for your healing.

MATTHEW 14:28–31; PHILIPPIANS 4:8

Prayer Declaration

Father, I have closed my mind to evil taunts and doubts of the enemy. No longer will I listen to him or allow my mind to be inhabited by his evil thoughts. I will fix my thoughts on You and on the healing that You have promised is available through the finished work of Your Son, Jesus, on the cross of Calvary.

SICKNESS DOES NOT COME FROM ME

MY DAUGHTER, SICKNESS does not come from Me—
sickness and disease are the works of the devil. I have made
a public spectacle of them and have triumphed over them. I
have established My kingdom on earth, and when My Son
walked on earth, He went everywhere preaching the message
of the kingdom and healing people. Healing accompanies
My kingdom. Remember that you do not have to be sick,
broke, poor, or confused any longer. Sickness and disease
are the works of the devil, and My Son came and disarmed
principalities and powers. He made a public spectacle of the
enemy and has triumphed over him.

COLOSSIANS 2:15; MATTHEW 4:23

Prayer Declaration

*Father, I thank You that in Your kingdom there is no sickness and
disease. Sickness and disease are works of the enemy, and I will not
be intimidated by him, for Jesus has taken all power and authority
from him. I will believe Your Word that promises that in His name
I can cast out demons and experience recovery from sickness.*

MY SON IS MOVED BY COMPASSION

WHEN MY SON walked among the people of earth and saw their need, He was moved with compassion for them. I care very deeply when My children suffer and hurt. I am a God full of compassion, and I will be gracious to My people. I am good to all My daughters, and My tender mercies are upon you. I will restore health unto you and will heal you of all your wounds. I sent My Son and anointed Him to preach the good news of the gospel to the poor, to heal the brokenhearted, to preach deliverance to the captives and recovering of sight to the blind, and to set at liberty them that are bruised. Those who are whole have no need of physician, but if you are sick, My daughter, I am come that you might have life and have it more abundantly.

PSALM 145:8–9; JEREMIAH 30:18; LUKE 4:18;
MATTHEW 9:12

Prayer Declaration

Jesus, thank You for caring so deeply about the things that can happen to Your people. Thank You for making it possible for me to live the abundant life that You promised. Thank You for healing me by Your stripes. Thank You for making a way for every sickness, ailment, illness, dysfunction, and disease to be healed and for me to be made whole.

I WILL HEAL ALL MANNER OF SICKNESS

MY SON HEALED *every* disease—with no exceptions. There was nothing too hard for Him. Do not let the enemy or your doctor tell you that you cannot be cured. It might be incurable to a doctor, but it's not incurable through the power and authority of My Son. My Son healed all who were sick, cast out the spirits with a word, and delivered many who were demon-possessed. When He sent His servants out, He gave them power against unclean spirits, to cast them out and to heal all manner of sickness and all manner of disease. He commanded them to give freely, for My Son gave freely to them. Stretch forth your hand to heal others, just as I have healed you. Show My people the signs and wonders that may be done in the name of My Son, Jesus.

MATTHEW 8:16; ACTS 4:30

Prayer Declaration

Father, I praise Your name because You do not want Your children to be sick or diseased or in pain. Thank You for filling my life with blessings and abundant life. It is not Your will for any to be in sickness and pain, and I will trust You for my healing—and for the healing of those to whom You send me with the message of Your kingdom.

MY SON BORE YOUR GRIEF AND SORROWS

MY SON WAS despised and rejected by men, a man of sorrows and acquainted with grief. He was despised, and the world did not esteem Him. My daughter, He bore your griefs and carried your sorrows. He was smitten and afflicted. He was wounded for your transgressions. He was bruised for your iniquities. The chastisement of your peace was upon Him, and by His stripes you are healed. But He rose victorious over sickness and disease and the grave, and through His death and resurrection He has purchased your salvation and healing.

ISAIAH 53:3–5

Prayer Declaration

Father, by the stripes of Jesus I am healed. He took my sickness; He carried my pain. I believe it is the will of God for me to be healed. When the sick and infirm came to Your Son, Jesus, on earth, He cast out the spirits with a word, and healed all who were sick. Because of Your great faithfulness to Your children, I place my trust in You that if they were healed then, so too will You heal us today.

FIND MY HEALING THROUGH LAYING ON HANDS

WHEN THE MULTITUDES who were sick and diseased came to My Son, He laid His hands on every one of them and healed them. When the woman who had a spirit of infirmity for eighteen years came to Him, unable to lift herself up, He called her to Him, laid hands on her, and immediately she was made straight. When My servant Paul saw that the father of one of his followers was sick, he prayed, laid his hands on him, and healed him. My healing virtue is available to My people through the laying on of hands. Trust in My ability to heal My people through the laying on of hands.

MATTHEW 19:15; LUKE 13:11–13; ACTS 28:8

Prayer Declaration

Father, let Your healing virtue flow to me and through me through the laying on of hands. Give me faith to believe in Your power, and show me those who are Your humble servants who can help me find my healing by laying hands on me. Equip me with Your power and authority so that I can meet the needs of those who come to me and ask me to pray for their healing.

OCTOBER 9

HEALING THROUGH DELIVERANCE

My daughter, the enemy afflicted many with his demonic spirits. The spirit of infirmity can operate by taking possession of people, as it did with the people My Son healed of evil spirits and infirmities, including Mary Magdalene. It is through the weakness of your fleshly nature that the gateway to the spirit of infirmity can enter in, possessing you and causing you to become a slave to uncleanness, lawlessness, and sin. But through your acceptance of the gift of salvation and healing offered through My Son, Jesus, you no longer have to be a slave to sin, but His power will deliver you from the enemy and set you free. But just as you were a slave to sin, so you must become a slave of righteousness for holiness. Having been set free from sin, you will produce the fruit of holiness and inherit everlasting life.

LUKE 8:2; ROMANS 6:19–22

Prayer Declaration

Forgive me, Lord, for allowing any fear, guilt, self-rejection, self-hatred, unforgiveness, bitterness, sin, pride, or rebellion to open the door to the spirit of infirmity. I renounce these things in the name of Jesus. In the name of Jesus I cast out any spirit of infirmity that came into my life through pride. I am no longer a slave to sin, but I have become a slave to righteousness, and I will produce the fruit of holiness in my life.

HEALING THROUGH BREAKING CURSES

THROUGH HIS SACRIFICE My Son has redeemed you from
the bondage of curses by becoming a curse for you on the cross
of Calvary. Many of the curses that affect My daughters have
entered their lives through inheritance—coming as a result of
the sins of their generations before them. But you are loosed
by all curses by My Son; live in your freedom and reject the
enemy who would want you to believe he still has control
over you. Rise up and use the authority you have through My
Son, and be loosed from all curses. Because of your faith in
Jesus, you have received the promise of My Spirit, and you are
empowered to walk in freedom and victory.

GALATIANS 3:13–14

Prayer Declaration

*Through the power of Christ I break all legal rights of all
generational spirits operating behind a curse in my life. I command all hereditary spirits of lust, rejection, fear, sickness, infirmity,
disease, anger, hatred, confusion, failure, and poverty to come out
of my life in the name of Jesus. Through Jesus my family is blessed.
I am free from the curse of sin, and I walk in freedom and victory.*

HEALING THROUGH ANOINTING OIL

MY SPIRIT AND anointing are what drive sickness and disease out of your body. The anointing oil breaks yokes of bondage, and sickness is a form of bondage. When My Son gave His servants power over unclean spirits and sent them out to loose the people from the power of the enemy, they anointed with oil many who were sick and healed them. My healing is available through the act of one of My servants anointing one who is sick. Are you sick? Call for the elders of My church, and let them pray over you, anointing you with oil in the name of My Son, and I will raise you up.

ISAIAH 10:27; MARK 6:10–13

Prayer Declaration

Father, just as Your Spirit anointed Jesus to preach the gospel, to heal the brokenhearted, and to preach deliverance to the captives, I will call for the elders to anoint me with oil through Your Spirit when I need healing. Give me the fullness of Your Spirit, Father, that I may be anointed to anoint those who need Your healing touch and free them from the bondage of sickness and infirmity.

HEALING THROUGH FAITH

MY DAUGHTER, DO not look at your sickness or the sickness of your loved ones as a mountain that cannot be moved. Have faith in Me. For assuredly I say to you, whoever says to this mountain, "Be removed and be cast into the sea," and does not doubt in her heart but believes that those things she says will be done, she will have whatever she says. Therefore I say to you, whatever things you ask when you pray, believe that you receive them, and you will have them. Do not turn and run when you are facing a mountain; stand and face your mountain and command: "Be thou removed." Rejoice when your faith is tested by the mountains of adversity, for the genuineness of your faith is much more precious than gold, and you shall receive the end of your faith—the salvation of your souls.

MARK 11:22–24; 1 PETER 1:18–21

Prayer Declaration

Father, I decree and declare that by faith I will face the mountains of sickness and adversity in my life and will command that they be removed. Because You have anointed me, I have faith and do not doubt that I can speak to any illness, curse it at the root, and cause it to be removed. I can tell the mountain of sickness that it is in my way and must move and be cast into the sea, and it shall be done.

Healing Through the Presence of God

When the leper was healed by My Son, the report of his healing spread abroad. Multitudes came together to hear My Son, and the power of His presence healed them. Let your praises rise to Me, for I will heal the brokenhearted and bind up their wounds. Invite My presence into your midst with your praise and worship, and My presence will bring deliverance and healing. I will make known to you the path of life and will fill you with joy in My presence. When you come into My presence, I will set your hearts at rest. Because you are My faithful servant, you can have confidence in Me and receive from Me whatever you ask. Therefore live in My presence, and I will be your sustenance in all things.

Luke 5:12–17; Psalm 147; 1 John 3:19–24

Prayer Declaration

Father, You have made known to me the path of life; You will fill me with joy in Your presence. There is power in Your presence to heal me and to deliver me from all my sickness and infirmity. Your Word has promised that those who have learned to acclaim You and who walk in the light of Your presence will rejoice in Your name all day long, and You will be their glory and strength.

HEALING THROUGH PRAYER

MY WORD PROMISES that all things, whatsoever you shall ask in prayer, believing, you shall receive. "All things" includes healing. My Word establishes the possibility of your healing in many ways. One of the ways I have established is through the anointing with oil by My servants. I have promised that the prayer of faith will save the sick, and it will also forgive your sin. But heed My Word that tells you to confess your trespasses to one another, and pray for one another, that you may be healed. The effective, fervent prayer of a righteous woman will avail much. Are you seeking to be healed? Come to Me with a humble heart, confess your sins, stand firm in your faith in My power, and wait in confidence for your healing to take place.

MATTHEW 21:22; JAMES 5:13–16

Prayer Declaration

Father, I have come before You with a humble heart, in need of Your healing touch. I confess my sins before You and accept Your gift of forgiveness through Your Son, Jesus. I will not be afraid of the spirit of sickness and infirmity that may be present in my body, for I stand in faith in the power of Your Holy Spirit and command the mountain of sickness to be removed from my life. My confidence in Your power to complete My healing is firm, and I wait patiently for You to respond to me with healing.

HEALING THROUGH THE GIFT OF HEALING

THE PRESENCE OF My Holy Spirit in your life will manifest through you in the power of the giftings He has placed within you, My daughter. My Spirit has placed His gifts within you for the profit of all—therefore exercise your gifting through His power. I have provided My healing for many through the gift of healing. If My Spirit has given it to you, it is because you are a part of My body, and all the parts of My body must work together. If one member suffers, all suffer with it, or if one member is honored, all the members rejoice with it. Therefore look with compassion upon your brothers and sisters who need a healing touch from Me through your gift of healing. Honor Me by honoring them, and offer My healing virtue to them by exercising your gifting.

1 CORINTHIANS 12

Prayer Declaration

Father, I have committed my life to You and have welcomed the presence of Your Holy Spirit into my life. Reveal to me the spiritual giftings that You have for me, and help me to have faith in the power and authority of Your Spirit to reach out and exercise my gifts for the profit of my brothers and sisters in Your body. Reveal Your power at work in me through the gift of healing, and let me offer Your healing touch to others through my gift.

HEALING THROUGH FASTING

In My Word I have told you that the acceptable day of fasting that I would choose for My people is when you fast to loose the bonds of wickedness, to undo the heavy burdens, to let the oppressed go free, and to break every yoke. My chosen fast for you is when you seek My face to prepare you with power and compassion to feed the hungry, clothe the naked, and separate yourself from your own fleshly nature. If You come to me in the spirit of fasting that is chosen by Me, then your light will break forth like the morning, and your healing will spring forth speedily. Your righteousness will go before you, and My glory will be your rear guard. Then you will call, and I will answer.

Isaiah 58:5–9

Prayer Declaration

Let me recognize that Your Word teaches me that sometimes there are answers I need from You that can come only through a time of prayer and fasting. Father, help me to call upon You for my healing through Your own chosen fast. Prepare me to fast as You have instructed in Your Word and to leave all other selfish motives far behind. Then You will hear My call and will cause my healing to spring forth speedily.

HEALING THROUGH THE WORD

WHEN MY PEOPLE called to Me in their time of trouble, I saved them out of their distresses and sent My Word and healed them and delivered them from their destructions. When My Word goes forth from My mouth, it will not return to Me void, but it will accomplish what I please and will prosper in the thing for which I sent it. My daughter, if I speak healing to you, then you will be healed. Learn to meditate on My Word and to learn from it so you know what I have said concerning your healing. My Word has declared that My right hand does valiantly, and you shall not die but live. Read My Word; confess My Word in your daily life. Concentrate on My healing scriptures. Trust Me for your healing, because My Word will accomplish in you all that I intend for it to accomplish.

ISAIAH 55:11; PSALM 118:17

Prayer Declaration

Father, my life and breath are in Your hands. You will show me the path of life. You will prolong my life and make my years as many generations. I will abide before You forever. Mercy and truth will preserve me. I will bless Your name and will not forget all Your benefits. You have forgiven my sins and healed all my diseases. You have redeemed my life from destruction. You satisfy me with good things, so that my youth is renewed like the eagle's.

HEALING THROUGH THE ANOINTING

I AM ABLE to work unusual miracles through My servants. When My Son, Jesus, walked on earth, the sick came to Him and begged Him that they might only touch the hem of His garment. And as many as touched it were made perfectly well. When cloth that had been touched by My servant Paul was brought to the sick and diseased, My healing anointing flowed through the touch of Paul to heal the sick and loose them from the evil spirits that had attacked them. Seek after My anointing power for your own healing. Call upon My humble servants to touch you so that My anointing can flow through them to you. Seek My Spirit to fill you with anointing so that you can reach out and pass My anointing power for healing on to those who need it.

MATTHEW 14:35–36; ACTS 19:12

Prayer Declaration

Father, I thank You that You can work in unusual ways and through unusual means to cause Your supernatural miracles to touch the lives of Your people. I want Your anointing to flow into me in any way You choose. Reveal to me the steps to my healing through Your anointing, and make me faithful to seek after Your power to heal.

Activate Your Faith

My DAUGHTER, YOU must desire Me with all your heart and soul. You must increase your faith, just as My Son's servants sought to increase their faith. Remember the words My Son said to them: "If you have faith as small as a mustard seed, you can say to this mulberry tree, 'Be uprooted and planted in the sea,' and it will obey you." Let words of praise be on your lips, that My peace be upon you and that I may heal you. I will restore health to you and heal you of all your wounds. Therefore press against the crowds, fight your way through traffic, and let no one stop you until you get into My presence. Hunger and thirst after My righteousness, and I will fill you.

Luke 17:5–6; Isaiah 57:19; Jeremiah 30:17; Mark 5:27–28

Prayer Declaration

O God, let me see You face-to-face so that my life will be preserved. I come to You in the midst of the multitude. I am hungrier for Your healing than for food. I feel Your compassion for me and know that You will heal me. I humble myself before You, O God. I pray and seek Your face. I turn from my wicked ways. Then I know You will hear from heaven and will forgive my sin and heal me.

PUT AWAY ANGER AND BITTERNESS

Do NOT ALLOW bitterness and anger to open the door for the spirit of infirmity to enter your life. Cease from anger and put away wrath to stay connected to Me. Speak soft words, kind words of life to turn wrath and anger away from you. Do not grieve another with your words. Give the bitterness of your soul to me. I will look upon your affliction and remember you. I will answer your petition and will send you on your way in peace. Diligently look within yourself, so that no bitter root can spring up to defile you.

PSALM 37:8–9; PROVERBS 15:1; 1 SAMUEL 1:10–11, 17; HEBREWS 12:15

Prayer Declaration

Father, my whole body is sick, and my health is broken because of my sins. But I confess my sins and am deeply sorry for what I have done. Do not abandon me, O Lord. Come quickly to help me, O Lord my Savior. Let all wrath and anger be put away from me. I will diligently look within myself so that no root of bitterness can defile me.

WALK IN FORGIVENESS

My HEART LONGS to forgive your sins and withhold My judgment from you. I will be merciful to you when you cry to Me, and I will bring joy to your soul. For I am good, and ready to forgive, and abundant in mercy to all those who call upon Me. From My dwelling place in heaven I will hear your prayers and supplications to Me, and I will maintain your cause. I will forgive your sins and trespasses and grant compassion to you in the midst of your enemies. My eyes are open to your supplications, and My ears will hear you when you call.

PSALM 86:3–4; 1 KINGS 8:49–50

Prayer Declaration

God, I thank You that when You hear prayers, You also forgive us. Forgive me of my sins and have compassion upon me. Like the servant who owed the king ten thousand talents, I too have been forgiven much. Therefore I will go and forgive all those who have sinned against me so that I will not be given over to the tormentors. With Your Son, Jesus, I pray, "Father, forgive them, for they do not know what they do."

OBEDIENCE IS A KEY

My daughter, I am love, and it is My desire that you walk in My love by following My instructions. Just as I promised My children of Israel, so I declare to you. If you obey My voice and do all that I speak, then I will be an enemy to your enemies and an adversary to your adversaries. I will go before you and will bring you into the land that I have chosen for you. If you serve Me with all your heart, I will bless your bread and water. I will take sickness away from the midst of you. I will fulfill the number of your days. I will make all your enemies turn their backs to you and will drive them out before you. I will give you My power and authority, and even the unclean spirits will obey you.

EXODUS 23:20–31; MARK 1:27

Prayer Declaration

Father, I am blessed because I obey Your Word to me. I will walk after Your ways and fear You and will keep Your Word. I will serve You and cleave to You. See how I love Your precepts and obey Your Word. Preserve my life, O Lord, according to Your love. I have confidence before You, Lord, for Your Word tells me that if I obey Your words and do what pleases You, then I will receive from You anything I ask.

You Have Authority in My Spirit

WHEN MY SON left the earth to return to Me, He prayed that My Holy Spirit would come to dwell among you. He guides you in all that you do, and My authority has been given to you through Him. If you believe in My Son, then You have the authority to do the works that He did—and even greater works—through My Spirit. If you ask anything in My name, I will do it. My grace is sufficient for you, for My power in you is made perfect in your weakness. Let My power strengthen you in your inner being through My Spirit. For I am able to do immeasurably more than all you ask or imagine, according to My power at work within you. For I did not give you a spirit of timidity, but a spirit of power and of love and of self-discipline.

JOHN 16:13; 2 CORINTHIANS 12:9; EPHESIANS 3:16–18; 2 TIMOTHY 1:7

Prayer Declaration

Father, I thank You that You did not give me a spirit of timidity, but of power and of love and of a sound mind. Your divine power and authority has given me everything I need for life and godliness through Your knowledge. You have given me Your great and precious promises, so that through them I can participate in Your divine nature, thus escaping the corruption of this world.

USE THE WISDOM I HAVE GIVEN TO YOU

MY DAUGHTER, JUST as I gave Solomon wisdom and exceedingly great understanding and largeness of heart like the sand on the seashore, so I will impart My wisdom unto you. My wisdom exceeds the wisdom of man. Let your mouth speak of My wisdom, and let the meditation of your heart be to understand My ways. Do not let sound wisdom or discretion depart from you, for they are life to your soul and grace to your neck. With them you will walk safely in all your ways, and your foot will not stumble. Let My spirit of wisdom and revelation increase your knowledge of Me. Let the eyes of your understanding be enlightened so you will know the hope of My calling and the riches of the glory of My inheritance to you.

1 KINGS 4:20–30; PSALM 49:3; PROVERBS 3:21–23;
EPHESIANS 1:17–18

Prayer Declaration

Let it not be up to me that I get rich through my own wisdom and understanding. Let my heart not be lifted up because of the world's riches, but let me humbly receive the wisdom and understanding that God gives, so that I will be made whole—body, mind, and spirit. I will ask God for any wisdom that I lack, and He will give it to me liberally.

Be Filled With My Wisdom From Above

Do you want to be wise and understanding? Then let Me see that your works are done in the meekness of My wisdom. Do not be consumed with the wisdom of this world, for it does not come from above. It is earthly, sensual, and demonic. My wisdom from above is first pure, then peaceable, gentle, willing to yield, full of mercy and good fruits, without partiality, and without hypocrisy. Let My Word dwell in you richly in all wisdom, teaching and admonishing one another in psalms and hymns and spiritual songs, singing with grace in your hearts to Me. Whatever you do in word or deed, do all in the name of My Son, Jesus, giving thanks to Me through Him.

James 3:13–17; Colossians 3:16–17

Prayer Declaration

May God give me the spirit of wisdom and revelation in the knowledge of Him. Let the eyes of my understanding be enlightened so I will know the hope of His calling and the riches of the glory of His inheritance. I thank You and praise You, God of my fathers, for You have given me wisdom and might. You have made known to me what I have asked of You.

FAITH RELEASES MY HEALING

WHEN MY SON asked the crowd who had touched Him, the woman who reached out to Him for healing fell down before Him. He said to her, "Daughter, your faith has made you well. Go in peace, and be healed of your affliction." My anointing power was activated by this woman's faith. Let your faith in Me for your healing grow strong like hers, and I will heal you. Faith releases My healing, and her faith drew healing power from My Son. When the multitudes of people brought the sick and laid them in the street for the shadow of Peter to fall on them when he passed by, it was because of their great faith that they were healed and delivered of unclean spirits. Build your faith, for through it you will activate My healing power.

MARK 5:32–34; ACTS 5:14–16

Prayer Declaration

Because You have anointed me, I have faith and do not doubt that I can speak to any illness, curse it at the root, and cause it to dry up and die, just as Your Son did to the fig tree. Because of faith I can tell the mountain of sickness that is in my way to move and be cast into the sea, and it shall be done. Lord, I believe; increase my faith.

I WILL RELEASE LIFE AND WHOLENESS INTO YOUR LIFE

DAUGHTER, LET YOUR heart be glad, and rejoice in Me. Let your flesh rest in hope, for I will not leave your soul in Sheol or allow you to see corruption. I will show you the path of life, and in My presence you will find fullness of joy. I will meet you with the blessings of goodness and give life and length of days to you when you ask. I will prolong your life and make your years as many generations. You will abide with Me forever, for My mercy and truth will preserve you.

PSALMS 16:1–11; 21:3–4; 61:6–7

Prayer Declaration

Father, You have granted me life and favor, and Your care has preserved my spirit. My life and breath are in Your hands. Goodness and mercy will follow me all the days of my life, and I will dwell in the house of the Lord forever. Your lovingkindness is better than life, and my lips will praise You. I will bless You while I live. I will lift up my hands in Your name.

RECOGNIZE HEALING POWER IN OTHERS

I HAVE BESTOWED My gift of healing on many of My daughters. Be careful to recognize My power at work, and show honor to those who possess My power. When My servant Elisha lived, many did not honor, respect, or receive his gifts—and did not receive the miracles they needed as a result. They had no faith. They did not honor My servant. My anointing for healing was available to them through Elisha, but they did not demand it from him. Yet when he lay in the tomb, a dead man was cast into his tomb, and when the man touched the bones of Elisha, he revived and stood up on his feet. Do not forget that the My Word and My power are in the mouth of My daughters.

2 KINGS 13:20 21; 1 KINGS 17:24

Prayer Declaration

The woman of God will pray for me, and I will be restored. I will make room in my home for her, so that she can be refreshed. I will follow the instructions that the woman of God gives me so that my flesh will be restored like that of a little child, and I will be clean. I will not stretch out my hand against the woman of God, for she is the Lord's anointed.

I Am Your Healer—Draw Close to Me

When the multitude pressed about My Son to hear the Word of God from Him, He got into a boat to put out a little from the land so that He could teach the multitudes My Word. Get closer to the Healer through My Word. Your hunger for the things of God will cause My Son to respond to You. He will never turn you away empty. Blessed are those who hunger and thirst for My righteousness, for they will be filled. Study to show yourself approved before Me, a laborer who does not need to be ashamed, rightly dividing My Word of truth. Come unto Me all you who labor and are heavy laden, and I will give you rest.

Luke 5:1–3; Matthew 5:6; 2 Timothy 2:15;
Matthew 11:28

Prayer Declaration

Father, I press in to touch You, for You are the Healer of all sickness. You will put forth Your hand to touch me. You will put Your life-giving and healing words in my mouth. You will teach me Your ways and increase my knowledge of You if I will study Your Word diligently. Lord, I long to get closer to You, for You are my healer.

PRAY MY WORD FOR YOUR HEALING

My daughter, give attention to My words; incline your ear to My sayings. Do not let them depart from your eyes; keep them in the midst of your heart. For they are life to those who find them, and health to all their flesh. Receive the pleasant words of My Word, for they are like a honeycomb, sweetness to your soul and health to your bones. My Word will cause you to prosper in all things and to be in health, just as your soul prospers. I have no greater joy than to know that you walk in My truths.

PROVERBS 4:20–22; 16:24; 3 JOHN 2–3

Prayer Declaration

Speak a word, Lord, and heal me this very hour. I will give attention to Your words. They will not depart from my eyes. I will keep them in the midst of my heart because they are life to me and health to my body. I declare that I prosper in all things and am in good health, just as my soul prospers.

OCTOBER 31

DRAW FROM THE WELL

WHEN MY SON met the woman of Samaria, He spoke to her of living water. Whoever drinks of My living water will never thirst. The water I give will become a fountain of water springing up into everlasting life. My daughter, draw deeply from My well of living water. There is a never-ending supply of My Spirit available to you if you will ask. Dig deep into the well of My Spirit, for I will make room for you and you will be fruitful in the land. Come and drink freely from the water that I have given to you. It is a well that springs up into everlasting life.

JOHN 4:13–14; PHILIPPIANS 1:19;
GENESIS 26:22; JOHN 4:14

Prayer Declaration

Father, You have opened my eyes to see the well of the water of Your Spirit. I will fill my cup and drink. I am fruitful by the well of Your Spirit. I abide in strength, and the arms of my hands are made strong by the hands of the almighty God. With joy I draw healing water out of the wells of salvation. A fountain of gardens, a well of living waters, and streams from Lebanon dwell within me.

NOVEMBER

Activating God's
Power

HEALING AND BLESSING FROM THE WATER OF LIFE

I WILL GIVE of the water of life freely to you when you thirst. As an overcomer, you will inherit all things from Me, and I will be your God, and you will be My daughter. I gave My servant John a foretaste of My water of life in My Word, and it too shall be for you. It is a pure river of water, providing food and drink for all nearby. When My water of life flows into your life, you will be like a tree planted by the waters. Your roots will spread out and your leaves will stay green. You will never cease to bear fruit in your life. You may come and drink of My water freely, for I am the fountain of life.

REVELATION 22:1–3, 17

Prayer Declaration

Father, I thirst, therefore I will come to You and drink living water. My belly overflows with rivers of living water because I believe in You. I am like a tree planted by the rivers of water. I bring forth fruit in my season. My leaves do not wither. Everything I do prospers. The Alpha and Omega, the beginning and the end, has given to me the fountain of the water of life freely, and I drink.

THIRST FOR MY LIVING WATER

REJOICE IN ME, My daughter, and come to Me when you are thirsty. I visit the earth and water it and greatly enrich it. My river is full of water and provides for the grain I give freely. I water the ridges abundantly and settle the furrows. I make it soft with showers and bless its growth. I will come down to you like the rain upon the grass before mowing and provide showers that water your thirsty places. I will turn your wilderness into pools of water and your dry land into watersprings. You will neither hunger nor thirst. The heat of the sun will not strike you. Be joyful, My daughter, for I will comfort you and have mercy on your afflictions.

PSALMS 65:9–10; 72:6; 107:35; ISAIAH 49:10–13

Prayer Declaration

As the deer pants after the water brooks, so my soul pants after You, O God. My soul thirsts for God, for the living God. My flesh longs for You in a dry and thirsty land where there is no water. You send Your water that flows out of the abundant river of God. Your water never runs dry, and it brings forth a bountiful harvest. You have turned the desert of my life into pools of water, and the dry ground into water springs. You make me dwell in fertile places. You bless me and multiply my seed greatly.

ACTIVATE YOUR HEALING GIFT

MY SON HAS given you His marching orders. Go and preach, telling My people that the kingdom of heaven is at hand. Heal the sick, cleanse the lepers, raise the dead, cast out demons. Freely you have received, freely give. Do not worry about how or what you should speak, for it is not you who speak, but My Spirit will speak through you. You have an anointing from My Holy Spirit, and He will enable you to know all things. His anointing will abide in you and will teach you concerning all things. My anointing is true, and not a lie, and will abide in you. I have anointed you for healing in your hands and body, and I will release My virtue through you. My supernatural miracles will flow through your life.

MATTHEW 10:7–8, 19–20; 1 JOHN 2:20–22

Prayer Declaration

Heavenly Father, I receive an anointing for healing in my hands and in my body. Let virtue be released through me. Let Your power be released through me so that wherever I go, people will be healed. I believe for miracles to flow through my life into the lives of others.

UNDERSTAND MY ANOINTING

BECAUSE I HAVE anointed you, My daughter, you can know all things. My anointing has endowed you with My Holy Spirit. This is My gift of supernatural power and ability. Through My gift you will receive healing, deliverance, and miracles, both for you and for those to whom I will send you. My healing virtue is available to you. If you have not, it is because you ask not. Ask Me for My anointing, and I will give it to you. Come boldly before My throne of grace in your hour of need, and I will activate My gift of healing through you. The works that My Son did you will do, and even greater than these.

1 JOHN 2:20–22, JAMES 4:2; JOHN 14:12

Prayer Declaration

I pray that You will anoint me to have Your healing virtue in my life—not only in my hands but also in my body. When I encounter sick people, they will be healed when I touch them because Your gift of healing flows through me. I will fast and pray and draw close to You. When I call upon You for Your healing virtue to flow, You will answer me in my hour of need, and Your miracles will flow through me.

SUBMIT YOURSELF TO SERVING ME

HEAR MY VOICE calling, My daughter. Whom shall I send, and who will go for Us? Submit yourself to serve Me, and I can send you to My people. For they keep on hearing but do not understand. They keep on seeing but do not perceive. I have anointed you and delivered you from the hands of your enemies, just as I called King David. I will make you like Stephen—full of faith and power—that I may do great wonders and miracles through you among My people. I have anointed you to open the eyes of My people in order to turn them from darkness into light and from the power of Satan to Me, that they may receive forgiveness of sins and an inheritance among those who are sanctified by faith in Me. Do not be disobedient to the heavenly vision, but declare My wonders among the people.

ISAIAH 6:8–9; 2 SAMUEL 12:7; ACTS 6:8; 26:17–19

Prayer Declaration

Father, I will answer Your call and will take the message of Your free gift of salvation wherever You send me. You are my strength, and I will praise Your wonders and tell of Your faithfulness also in the congregation of the saints. Make me full of faith and power like Stephen. You have called me, and You are faithful to do through me that for which I was called.

PRAY FOR PERSONAL ANOINTING

I HAVE FILLED you with My Holy Ghost and with faith so that many will see your anointing and will be added unto My body because of your ministry. I have enabled you and have counted you faithful to be My spokeswoman. I have given you the power of My Spirit and am sending you forth to your city, your region, and throughout the world. Follow My anointing power, and you will reap a harvest of My fruit—My love, joy, peace, long-suffering, gentleness, goodness, faith, meekness, and temperance—that draws others to demand My anointing for themselves. I have called you, and I am faithful to do through you that for which I called you.

ACTS 11:24; GALATIANS 5:22–23, 1 TIMOTHY 1:12

Prayer Declaration

*I will stay full of the Holy Ghost and of faith so that many will
be added unto the body of Christ. I have been anointed
to open their eyes and to turn them from darkness to
light and from the power of Satan unto God, that they
may receive forgiveness of sins and inheritance among
those who are sanctified by the faith that is in me.*

I Will Release Generational Anointing

Just as I anointed Aaron and his sons after him, so you have been anointed and consecrated—you and your children— for service to Me. I am raising you up a faithful priest, My daughter, and you will do according to what is in My heart and mind for you to do. I will be your tower of salvation and will show My mercy to you. I will bless your children. Have faith in Me for what I will do in them and through them in the future. I will cover your children with the blood of Jesus, and the angel of death will not touch them, but pass over. Because of My anointing on your life, I will grant all your future generations great deliverance and mercy.

Exodus 29:29; 1 Samuel 2:35; Psalm 18:50

Prayer Declaration

Lord, I believe that I have been anointed by You just as You anoint- ed my fathers, that I may minister unto You in my ministry gifting and that my family may be an everlasting priesthood throughout all our generations. I offer You my children and declare them to be Yours. In faith I receive Your promises for my life and for theirs.

I Have Revealed My Covenant Plan

WHEN MY SON established My kingdom upon the earth, He declared that it would reach to all peoples—Jew and Gentile alike. My kingdom is for all, and it will rebuild and establish My tabernacle among mankind, so that all may seek Me and enter in. My kingdom is a new-covenant body—My church. It will fill My people with everlasting joy and will be a covenant of peace. My daughter, I have called you into the kingdom and clothed you in My righteousness through My Son. Let My righteousness, peace, and joy increase in your life and spread through all your generations.

ACTS 15:12–17; ISAIAH 61:1–3; HEBREWS 12:22;
ISAIAH 54:10; EPHESIANS 4:24

Prayer Declaration

Lord, may I be able to say, "I have proclaimed glad tidings of righteousness in the great congregation; behold, I will not restrain my lips. O Lord, You know I have not hidden Your righteousness within my heart; I have spoken of Your faithfulness and Your salvation. I have not concealed Your loving-kindness and Your truth from the people who need to be brought into Your kingdom."

I HAVE BROUGHT YOU INTO MY KINGDOM

MY DAUGHTER, THE kingdom of God—My kingdom—is within you. In My kingdom the righteous will flourish, and the earth will be filled with the knowledge of My ways. I long for My kingdom to spread over the earth, but whom shall I send, and who will go for Me to bring the world into My kingdom? Like My servant Isaiah, will you go for Me? My greatness is unsearchable; declare My mighty acts and My awesome deeds and greatness. Sing of My righteousness, for I am gracious and full of compassion and good to all. Speak of the glories of My kingdom, for it is an everlasting kingdom that endures throughout all generations. Depart from those who harden their hearts and will not listen, and reason daily with all who hear the Word and will accept My ways.

LUKE 17:21; PSALM 145:1–13; ACTS 19:6–10

Prayer Declaration

Your throne, O God, is forever and ever; You hold a scepter of righteousness in Your hand and anoint Your people with the oil of gladness. You are clothed with honor and majesty. You walk on the wings of the wind and make the clouds Your chariot. How manifold are Your works; the earth is full of Your possessions. I will sing praise to You while I have my being, and I will show forth Your wonders to all Your people.

THERE IS GREAT JOY IN MY KINGDOM

DAUGHTER, MY KINGDOM is filled with great joy and rejoicing. The wilderness and the wasteland shall be glad, and the desert shall rejoice and blossom as the rose. It shall blossom abundantly and rejoice, even with joy and singing. My redeemed will walk in My kingdom, and the ransomed of the Lord will return and come to Zion with singing, with everlasting joy on their heads. They will obtain joy and gladness, and sorrow and sighing will flee away. Let the peoples praise Me, and let the nations be glad and sing for joy. I will judge My people righteously and govern the nations on earth. Remember My loving-kindness, and rejoice and be glad, for I will be Your God forever and ever.

ISAIAH 35:1–2, 10; PSALM 67:3–4

Prayer Declaration

I will clap my hands and shout to God with cries of joy. How awesome You are, O Most High, the great King over all the earth. You subdue nations and have chosen Your kingdom as our inheritance. You have ascended amid shouts of joy and the sounding of trumpets. I will sing praises to my King. For You are the King of all the earth; You reign over the nations. You are seated on Your holy throne, and the kings of the earth belong to You and greatly exalt Your name.

MY SON IS THE PRINCE OF PEACE

MY SON CAME as a child to establish His kingdom. The government will be upon His shoulder. And His name will be called Wonderful, Counselor, Mighty God, Everlasting Father, Prince of Peace. Of the increase of His government and peace there will be no end. He will rule over the throne of David and over his kingdom, to order it and establish it with judgment and justice, from that time forward, even forever. Open the gates that the righteous may enter, the nation that keeps faith. I will keep you in perfect peace if your mind is steadfast in Me. Trust in Me, My daughter, for I am the Lord, the Rock Eternal. Let the peace of My Son rule in your heart, for I have called you to peace.

ISAIAH 9:6–7; 26:2–3; COLOSSIANS 3:15

Prayer Declaration

In Your kingdom, Lord, You will extend peace like a river and a flowing stream to all peoples. You will comfort Your people, and our hearts will rejoice. I will lie down and sleep in peace, for You alone, O Lord, make me dwell in safety. Let righteousness work peace in my life, and let the effect of righteousness be quietness and confidence forever.

THE RIGHTEOUS WILL REIGN WITH ME

I WILL REIGN in My kingdom in righteousness, and My righteous people will rule with justice. For if You died with My Son, you shall also live with Him. If you endure, you shall also reign with Him. For He has redeemed you to God by His blood, those from every tribe and tongue and people and nations, and has made you kings and priests to Me, and you will reign on the earth. My rule will extend from sea to sea, and from the river to the ends of the earth. As for you, because of the blood of My Son, I will free you and will proclaim peace to the nations.

ISAIAH 32:1; 2 TIMOTHY 2:12; REVELATION 5:10;
ZECHARIAH 9:10

Prayer Declaration

Lord, the heavens declare Your glory, and the skies proclaim the work of Your hands. Lord, You let us rule everything Your hands have made. And You put all of it under our power— the sheep and the cattle, and every wild animal, the birds in the sky, the fish in the sea, and all ocean creatures. Our Lord and Ruler, Your name is wonderful everywhere on earth.

MY KINGDOM IS A KINGDOM OF RIGHTEOUSNESS

MY KINGDOM IS a kingdom of righteousness, and I hold the scepter of righteousness in My hand. I will lead you in the paths of righteousness. If you will trust in Me, I will bring forth your righteousness as the light. Those who wait upon Me will inherit the earth and will delight themselves in the abundance of peace. Blessed is the woman I choose and cause to approach Me. You will dwell in My courts and be satisfied with the goodness of My house. I will answer you with awesome deeds of righteousness, and I establish the mountains by My strength. The work of righteousness will be peace, and the effect of righteousness will be quietness and assurance forever.

PSALM 23:3; ISAIAH 32:17

Prayer Declaration

You have called us to righteousness, O Lord, and You will hold me in Your hand. You will give me as a covenant to the people, as a light to the Gentiles. Through You I will open blind eyes and bring prisoners out from the prison, even those who sit in darkness in the prison house. Surely in You I have righteousness and strength. For this is the heritage of the servants of the Lord, and my righteousness will come from You.

I Have Planted You in Righteousness

I HAVE COME to proclaim the establishment of My kingdom—a kingdom of righteousness. I will comfort and console you when you mourn, daughter, and I will give you beauty for ashes and the oil of joy for mourning. I will clothe you in the garment of praise for the spirit of heaviness, that you may be called a tree of righteousness, My planting, that you may glorify Me. You will eat the riches of the heathen, and instead of shame you will have double honor. Everlasting joy will be yours. I will make with you an everlasting covenant. Your descendants will be known among the heathen, for they are the posterity that I have blessed. I will cause righteousness and praise to spring forth before all the nations.

ISAIAH 61

Prayer Declaration

Lord, let me be clothed with righteousness. Let righteousness work peace in my life, and let the effect of righteousness be quietness and confidence forever. You give me beauty for ashes, the oil of joy for mourning, the garment of praise for the spirit of heaviness, that I may be called a tree of righteousness, Your planting, that You may be glorified.

I AM FILLING THE WORLD WITH MY RIGHTEOUSNESS

I WILL MAKE My salvation known and will reveal My righteousness to the nations. I work righteousness and justice for all the oppressed. My throne is established in mercy, and I sit upon it in truth in the tabernacle of David, judging and seeking justice and hastening righteousness. The heavens will rain down and the skies will pour down righteousness. The earth will open and bring forth salvation, and righteousness will spring up together. Righteousness and praise will spring forth before all nations. The nations will see My righteousness, and all kings My glory. I will fill the world with My righteousness.

ISAIAH 16:5; 45:8; 62:2

Prayer Declaration

I will go in the strength of the Lord. I will make mention of Your righteousness, of Yours only. I am established in righteousness, and tyranny will be far from me. I will have nothing to fear, for terror will be far removed and will not come near me. I will delight greatly in You, O Lord; my soul will rejoice in You. You have clothed me with garments of salvation and arrayed me in a robe of righteousness.

MY SON, JESUS, IS YOUR MESSIAH-KING

THE ESTABLISHMENT OF My kingdom was accomplished through My Son—your Messiah-King. Let all the nations rejoice and sing, for He shall judge the people righteously and govern the nations on earth. He will bring peace to all in His kingdom and ordain peace for His people. He was anointed by Me to bring the message of the kingdom and to establish it on earth. Of the increase of His government and peace there will be no end. His kingdom is from generation to generation. The gospel is a declaration of His reign.

PSALM 67:5; ISAIAH 55:5; MARK 1:15

Prayer Declaration

How beautiful upon the mountains are the feet of her who brings good news, who proclaims peace, who brings glad tidings of good things, who proclaims salvation, and who says to Zion, "Your God reigns!"

GIVE YOURSELF TO THE PREACHING
OF THE GOSPEL

MY KINGDOM WILL come to the heathen through your preaching of the gospel. Go into all the world and preach the good news to all creation. Whoever believes and is baptized will be saved, but whoever does not believe will be condemned. I have commanded you to preach to the people and testify that My Son is the one whom I appointed as judge of the living and the dead. I have given you grace to preach the unsearchable riches of My Son's kingdom and to make plain to everyone the mystery of the kingdom. Through this all will know My manifold wisdom, according to My eternal purpose that I accomplished through My Son. In Him and through Him you may approach Me with freedom and confidence.

PSALM 47:8; MARK 16:15; ACTS 10:42;
EPHESIANS 3:8–12

Prayer Declaration

Father, I will answer Your call to preach the gospel to all people. I am not ashamed of the gospel, because it is the power of God for the salvation of everyone who believes: first for the Jew, then for the Gentile. For in the gospel a righteousness from God is revealed, a righteousness that is by faith from first to last, just as it is written: "The righteous will live by faith."

UNDERSTAND THE MYSTERIES OF
MY KINGDOM

MY DAUGHTER, THE mysteries, the secrets, of the kingdom of heaven have been given to you. I have entrusted you with the secret things of My kingdom. Prove yourself faithful, for I will judge you for your faithfulness. I will bring to light what is hidden in darkness and will expose the motives of men's hearts. The mysteries of My kingdom are made known to you that you may reveal them to all people so that they can become fellow heirs of My body and partakers of the promises of the kingdom through Christ. This revelation is given to you by the gift of the grace of God, which is given to you through the effective working of His power. It is My will to make known the riches of the glory of My kingdom to all people.

1 CORINTHIANS 4:1–5; EPHESIANS 3:1–7;
COLOSSIANS 1:27

Prayer Declaration

Father, thank You for entrusting me with the revelation of the mysteries of Your kingdom. Through Your Son, Jesus, and Your Holy Spirit within me, You have anointed me to preach good news to the poor. You have sent me to proclaim freedom for the prisoners and recovery of sight for the blind, to release the oppressed, to proclaim the year of the Lord's favor.

I HAVE A GLORIOUS PLAN FOR THE GENTILES

IT IS MY plan that My kingdom would have dominion over all the peoples of the world. Through My Son I confirmed the promises made to Abraham, that the Gentiles might glorify Me for My mercy toward them. Isaiah spoke to My people to confirm this promise when he said, "There shall be a root of Jesse, and He shall rise to reign over the Gentiles. In Him the Gentiles shall have hope." My light has come to all people, and My glory rises upon them. The Gentiles will come to My light, and kings to the brightness of My rising. They will gather together and come to Me. Then they will see and become radiant, and their hearts will swell with joy.

PSALM 72:8; ROMANS 15:12; ISAIAH 60:1–5

Prayer Declaration

Father, Your Word has revealed that You will justify all nations by faith and bless all nations through Your promise to Abraham. Wherever I open my mouth, may Your words be given to me so that I fearlessly may know the mystery of Your kingdom. For through Jesus You are able to establish me by the gospel, so that I may proclaim the mystery of Your kingdom, hidden in times past, but now revealed and made known so that all nations might believe and obey You.

I Am Subduing the Nations

THE WORK OF My kingdom is triumphant, and I rule as King over all the earth. I will subdue the peoples under My kingdom, and the nations under it. I will go before you and make the crooked places straight. I will break the bars of bronze and cut the bars of darkness. I will give you the treasures of darkness and the hidden riches of My kingdom, that you may know that I have called My people by name, even before they know Me. I am the Lord, and there is no other. I will do all things. I will rain down My blessings from heaven and let the skies pour down My righteousness. The earth will open and bring forth salvation, and righteousness and salvation will reign together upon the earth.

ISAIAH 45:1–8

Prayer Declaration

You are the Lord Most High, the great King over all the earth. You will subdue the peoples under Your kingdom. You reign over the nations; You sit upon the throne of Your holiness. Let the nobles of the nations assemble as the people of the God of Abraham, for the kings of the earth belong to You. Let the people, all the inhabitants of the world, hear and understand Your parables of the kingdom.

THE OLD COVENANT PROMISES ARE FULFILLED THROUGH MY SON

THROUGH MY SON the promises of My old covenant with My people have been fulfilled. All the ends of the earth will remember and turn to Me, and all the families of the nations will worship Me. For the kingdom is Mine, and I rule over the nations. My way will be known on earth, and My salvation among all nations. The nations will be glad and sing for joy. All the nations that I have made will come and worship before Me and will glorify My name. Wherever the people are submitting their hearts to the rule of My Son, the King of the kingdom, I will release heaven on earth.

PSALMS 22:27–28; 67:2, 4; 86:9; HEBREWS 12:22

Prayer Declaration

Father, I praise You that through the work of Your Son, Jesus, You have established Your kingdom on earth and have opened the gates of the kingdom for all the nations of the world. I will diligently pray and work to see Your kingdom fulfilled in all the nations of my world.

Worship Me in Spirit and Truth

In the days of My old covenant with Israel, My people would come in the temple to meet with Me and to worship Me. Through My Son the veil of separation between Me and My people has been removed, and My people now worship Me in Spirit and truth. I am seeking for true worshippers who will worship Me in spirit and truth, for I am Spirit, and those who worship Me must worship in spirit and truth. Behold My Son, in whom My soul delights. I have put My Spirit upon Him, and He will bring forth justice to all people. He will bring forth justice for truth. He will not fail or be discouraged until He has established justice in the earth.

John 4:22–24; Isaiah 42:1–9

Prayer Declaration

Father, no longer do we approach You through a veil of darkness, but through Jesus we have access to Your throne of grace. You placed Your Spirit upon Him, and You anointed Him to preach good tidings unto the meek. You sent Him to bind up the brokenhearted and to proclaim liberty to the captives and the opening of the prison to them that are bound. He will comfort all who mourn and will place the garment of praise on Your people. We will be trees of righteousness, the planting of Your Son, so that He might be glorified.

My Kingdom Is Not of This World

My KINGDOM IS not of this world. My kingdom is not eating and drinking, but it is righteousness and peace and joy in My Holy Spirit. For she who serves My Son in these things is acceptable to Me and approved by men. Therefore pursue the things that make for peace and the things that edify one another. Do not do anything that causes your sister to stumble or be offended. Entrance into My kingdom does not come by physical birth; it can only be entered into by spiritual birth. My kingdom exists within My people. My kingdom is like a river flowing from Zion to the nations. Wherever the rivers goes, it brings healing.

ROMANS 14:17–21; LUKE 17:21; EZEKIEL 47

Prayer Declaration

Father, You have established Your throne in heaven, and Your kingdom rules over all. Let men speak of the glory of Your kingdom and talk of Your power. Your kingdom does not come with observation; it is not physical, but it exists within Your people. Your kingdom is not meat and drink, but righteousness, peace, and joy in Your Holy Spirit.

I Have Placed My Kingdom Within You

DAUGHTER, DO NOT think like those who believed that the promised Messiah would come to earth to establish a kingdom that could be observed in the natural. For the kingdom does not come with observation. For indeed My kingdom is within you. My Son established My kingdom through His death and resurrection, and I have placed My Holy Spirit within you to establish My kingdom in your heart. If you confess your faith in My Son with your mouth and believe in your heart that God has raised Him from the dead, you will be saved and will become a part of My kingdom. Strengthen your hearts in faith to pray diligently that My kingdom will be established in fullness throughout the world.

LUKE 17:20–21; ROMANS 10:9–10

Prayer Declaration

Father, thank You for the work of Your Son, who came to establish Your kingdom on earth. Help me to understand the mysteries of Your kingdom and to comprehend fully that Your kingdom dwells within the hearts of Your people. Teach me to build up my faith and to work diligently to make known Your kingdom to all people. We long for the day when You will come again and establish Your kingdom in its fullness upon the earth.

My Son Is Set Upon the Holy Hill of Zion

I HAVE SET My King on My holy hill of Zion and have decreed: "You are My Son, whom I have begotten. Ask of Me, and I will give you the nations for Your inheritance and the ends of the earth for Your possessions." My Son will rule My kingdom from Zion; therefore blessed are you if you put your trust in Him. He will answer you in the day of trouble and will defend you and send help to strengthen you from His holy throne in Zion. He has chosen Zion for His dwelling place, and all who enter His kingdom will dwell in Zion. He will abundantly bless His people with provision and satisfy the poor with bread. He will clothe His priests with salvation, and the saints will shout aloud for joy. He will clothe His enemies with shame, but His crown will flourish and His kingdom live eternally.

PSALMS 2:7–8; 20:1–2; 132:13–18

Prayer Declaration

Lord, You have been set upon the holy hill of Zion, and You will rule in the midst of Your enemies. I praise You that I will dwell in Zion. I will sing praises unto You and declare Your doing among the people. Your salvation has come out of Zion, and You have brought back the captivity of Your people. I bless You, for You have shown me Your marvelous kindness in a strange city. Let Zion be established forever.

MY SON IS THE RULER OF ALL

THE KINGDOM IS My Son's, and He rules over the nations. He rules by His power forever. His eyes observe the nations, and He will not let the rebellious exalt themselves. He will keep your soul among the living and will not allow your feet to be moved. He will test His people and refine them as silver is refined. Though you go through fire and through water, My daughter, He will bring you out to rich fulfillment. My Son loves justice and has established equity. He executes justice and righteousness. He will act wisely, and He will be raised and lifted up and highly exalted. Psalm 56:7–12

Prayer Declaration

Lord, You let us rule everything Your hands have made. And You put all of it under our power—the sheep and the cattle, and every wild animal, the birds in the sky, the fish in the sea, and all ocean creatures. Our Lord and Ruler, Your name is wonderful everywhere on earth! Lord, everyone on this earth will remember You. People all over the world will turn and worship You, because You are in control, the ruler of all nations.

FOLLOW MY PATH OF RIGHTEOUSNESS

MY DAUGHTER, IF you receive My words and treasure My commands within you, so that you incline your ear to wisdom and apply your heart to understanding, yes, if you cry out for discernment and lift up your voice for understanding, if you seek her as silver and search for her as for hidden treasures, then you will understand the fear of the Lord and find My knowledge. For I give wisdom; from My mouth come knowledge and understanding; I store up sound wisdom for the upright; I am a shield to those who walk uprightly. I guard the path of righteousness and preserve the way of My saints.

PROVERBS 2:1–8

Prayer Declaration

Father, this is the prayer of my heart: "Open for me the gates of righteousness; I will enter and give thanks to the Lord. This is the gate of the Lord through which the righteous may enter. I will give You thanks, for You answered me; You have become my salvation." I will go in the strength of the Lord God; I will make mention of Your righteousness, of Yours only.

LISTEN FOR MY VOICE ABOVE ALL OTHERS

I AM THE God of glory and strength. My voice can be heard over the thunder of mighty waters, for it is powerful and majestic. It can split a mighty cedar or flash with the lightning. It can shake the desert and strip the forests bare. I will cause My enemies to hear My voice and will shatter My enemies. Yet I can speak with My daughters with a still, small voice, a gentle whisper, as I did with My servant Elijah, and give them counsel, consolation, and instruction. My daughter, learn to listen to My voice and to know My voice as sheep know the voice of their shepherd. If you diligently obey My voice and observe carefully all My instructions, then I will bless your life because you obey My voice. I will bring you back from captivity and have compassion on you.

PSALM 29:3–9; 1 KINGS 19:10–18; DEUTERONOMY 28

Prayer Declaration

Lord, the heavens declare Your glory, and the skies proclaim the work of Your hands. Your voice has gone out into all the earth, and Your words to the ends of the world. I hear the voice of the Lord. He tells me the way, when I should turn to the right or to the left, and counsels me to walk in the way. Speak to me, Lord, and I will listen and will obey Your voice.

Delight Yourself in Me

Delight yourself in Me, and I will give you the desires of your heart. Commit your way to Me; trust in Me, and I will do this. I will make your righteousness shine like the dawn, the justice of your cause like the noonday sun. Be still and wait patiently for Me. Do not fret when men succeed in their ways and carry out their wicked schemes. For those who hope in Me will inherit the land. I delight in those who know and understand Me, that I am the Lord who exercises kindness, justice, and righteousness on earth. I am with you; never again will you fear any harm. Do not let your hands hang limp, for I am with you. I am mighty to save, and I take great delight in you, My daughter. I will quiet you with My love and rejoice over you with singing.

Psalm 37:4–9; Jeremiah 9:24; Zephaniah 3:15–18

Prayer Declaration

I delight greatly in the Lord; my soul rejoices in my God. For He has clothed me with garments of salvation and arrayed me in a robe of His righteousness, as a bridegroom adorns his head like a priest and as a bride adorns herself with her jewels. For as the soil makes the sprout come up and a garden causes seeds to grow, so the sovereign Lord will make righteousness and praise spring up before all nations.

GIVE YOUR WORSHIP AND PRAISE TO ME

My KINGDOM WILL be known throughout the whole world. People from every nation will come to dwell forever in My kingdom, and the nations of the world will give praise and worship to My name and will glorify Me. I will be the hope of the Gentiles. The kings and judges of the earth will be wise and will serve Me with reverent awe and worshipful fear and rejoice with trembling. They will worship before Me in the beauty of holiness and sing praises unto Me.

ROMANS 15:9–12; PSALMS 2:10–11; 66;4

Prayer Declaration

Lord, everyone on this earth will remember You. People all over the world will turn and worship You, because You are in control, the ruler of all nations. I will worship at Your altar because You make me joyful. You are my God, and I will praise You.

DECEMBER

God Is the Fulfillment
of My Life

I AM A GOD IN WHOM YOU CAN TRUST

THE NATIONS AND people of the world will offer the sacrifice of righteousness to Me and put their trust in Me. I am their strength and shield; they will trust in Me with their hearts, and I will help them. Therefore they will greatly rejoice and praise Me with song. They will abide in My tabernacle forever and will trust in the shelter of My wings. I will be their salvation. They will trust and not be afraid, for I am the Lord God Jehovah and have become their strength and their song. I will keep them in perfect peace because their minds are stayed on Me and they trust in Me.

PSALMS 28:7; 61:4; ISAIAH 26:3

Prayer Declaration

Cause me to hear Your loving-kindness in the morning, for in You do I trust; cause me to know the way in which I should walk, for I lift up my soul to You. Lord, I trust in You. Let me be as a tree planted by the waters that spreads my roots by the river, so I need not fear when heat comes. Let my leaf be green, and keep me worry-free in the year of drought, never failing to bear fruit.

I Will Satisfy Your Soul

I WILL SATISFY My daughters with long life and show My salvation. I will satisfy your desires with good things, so that your youth is renewed like the eagle's. I will satisfy your soul with abundance and fill you with goodness. I will guide you continually. You will be like a watered garden and like a spring of water, whose waters fail not. I will bless your provision and satisfy you with bread.

PSALMS 103:5; 91:16; JEREMIAH 31:14; ISAIAH 58:11;
PSALM 132:15

Prayer Declaration

*Lord, You are my refuge and my fortress, my God, in whom
I trust. Surely You will save Me from the fowler's snare
and from the deadly pestilence. You will cover me with
Your feathers, and under Your wings I will find refuge;
Your faithfulness will be my shield and rampart. With long
life You will satisfy me and show me Your salvation.*

GOD IS THE FULFILLMENT OF MY LIFE

I WILL HIDE YOU FROM THE WICKED

I WILL PROTECT your life from the threat of the enemy and hide you from their wicked conspiracies and plots. Surely I will shoot them with My arrows, and they will suddenly be struck down. I will provide a place for you, My daughter, and will plant you so that you have a home of your own and will no longer be disturbed. Wicked people will not oppress you anymore. I will watch over the ways of My righteous daughters, but the way of the wicked leads to destruction. Though they plot evil against you and devise wicked schemes, they cannot succeed.

PSALM 64:1–2; 1 CHRONICLES 17:9; PSALMS 1:6; 21:11

Prayer Declaration

Lord, lift up the humble, but cast the wicked to the ground. Hide me from the secret plot of the wicked, from the rebellion of the workers of iniquity. I will be still before You and wait patiently for You, for the power of the wicked will be broken, but You will uphold the righteous. You are a just God and will not forsake Your faithful ones. Wrongdoers will be completely destroyed, and the offspring of the wicked will perish.

MY WORKS ARE AWESOME

MY DAUGHTER, I am the Lord Most High, and My works are awesome. I am a great King over all the earth. I will subdue the peoples under Me and the nations under My feet. I will answer you when you call upon Me, and I will reward My people with awesome deeds of righteousness. Through the greatness of My power your enemies will submit themselves to Me. Men shall speak of the might of My awesome acts and will declare My greatness.

PSALMS 47:2–3; 65:5; 66:3; 145:6

Prayer Declaration

Father, You are the Lord Most High and are awesome in Your deeds. You are the great King over all the earth. You will subdue the peoples under us and the nations under our feet. I will speak of the might of Your acts and will declare Your greatness. You, Lord, are all I want! You are my choice, and You keep me safe. You make my life pleasant, and my future is bright.

MY NAME WILL ENDURE FOREVER

I AM A great God, greater than all the gods. My name will endure forever, and My renown through all generations. I will vindicate My people and have compassion on My servants. I will do whatever pleases Me in the heavens and on the earth, in the seas and all their depths. I make clouds rise from the ends of the earth and send lightning with the rain. Of the increase of My government and peace there will be no end. I will establish My kingdom and will order it and establish it with judgment and justice forever. My name will endure forever and shall continue as long as the sun. Men will be blessed in Me, and all nations will call Me blessed.

PSALMS 135:3–7, 13–14; 72:17

Prayer Declaration

Father, blessed are those who have learned to acclaim You, who walk in the light of Your presence, O Lord. They rejoice in Your name all day long; they exult in Your righteousness. For You are their glory and strength. All nations whom You have made shall come and worship before You, O Lord, and shall glorify Your name.

DECLARE MY GLORY

THE HEAVENS DECLARE My glory; the skies proclaim the works of My hands. Declare My glory among the nations and My marvelous deeds among all peoples. I am worthy to receive glory and honor and power, for I created all things, and by My will they were created and have their being. Bring glory to My name, for I alone am holy. All nations will come and worship before Me, for My righteous acts have been revealed.

PSALM 19:1; 1 CHRONICLES 16:24

Prayer Declaration

Yours, Lord, is the greatness and the power and the glory and the majesty and the splendor, for everything in heaven and earth is Yours. Yours, Lord, is the kingdom; You are exalted as head over all. How majestic is Your name in all the earth. You have set Your glory in the heavens.

I Reign Over All

LET THE EARTH be glad, for I reign. Let the distant shores rejoice. The heavens proclaim My righteousness, and all the people will see My glory. I have made My salvation known and revealed My righteousness to the nations. I remember My love and faithfulness to My people; all the ends of the earth will see My salvation. I reign above all; I am clothed with majesty and robed with strength and power. I have established the world, and it cannot be moved.

PSALMS 97:1; 98:1–3; 93:1

Prayer Declaration

You have revealed Your righteousness to us, and I will proclaim Your salvation to all who need to hear of it. I will raise my voice to the nations and speak of Your majesty and strength and power. I will proclaim Your love and faithfulness wherever I go.

I WILL HEAR YOUR PRAYER

MY DAUGHTER, WHEN you call on Me, I will answer you. I will turn My ear to your prayer and show you the wonders of My great love. I will keep you as the apple of My eye and hide you in the shadow of My wings from the wicked who are out to destroy you. I will rise up and confront your enemies and bring them down. I will rescue you from the wicked with My sword and save you from such people. My eyes are on the righteous, and My ears are attentive to their prayer. But My face is against those who do evil.

PSALM 17:6–9, 13–14; 1 PETER 3:12

Prayer Declaration

You have heard my supplication and will receive my prayer. You have said that You will answer my prayers and have set a time when You will come to save me. You will hear the prayer of the destitute and will not despise their prayer. You will hear the groaning of the prisoner and will release those appointed to death. Before I call, You will answer, and while I am speaking, You will hear.

I Will Remove Your Sins

I AM COMPASSIONATE and gracious, slow to anger, abounding in love. I will not always accuse, nor will I harbor My anger forever. I do not treat you as your sins deserve or repay you according to your iniquities. As far as the east is from the west, so far have I removed your transgressions from you. As a father has compassion on his children, so I have compassion on those who fear Me; I know how you are formed, and I remember that you are dust. From everlasting to everlasting My love is with those who fear Me, and My righteousness with your children's children—with those who keep My covenant and remember to obey My precepts.

PSALM 103:13–18

Prayer Declaration

You have taken me out of the nations and gathered Your people from all the countries and brought us back into Your own land. You have sprinkled clean water on us, and we are clean; You have cleansed us from all our impurities and from all our idols. You have given me a new heart and put a new spirit in me. You have removed my heart of stone and given me a heart of flesh. You have put Your Spirit in me and moved me to follow Your decrees and to be careful to keep Your laws. I will live in the land You gave Me. I will be Your child, and You will be My God.

I WILL BLESS YOUR PROVISION

I HAVE BLESSED your provision and satisfied you with bread. I have blessed you and surrounded your life with favor. My showers of blessing will be released upon your life in season. I will bless the fruit of your womb, the crops of your land, and your livestock. Your basket and your kneading trough will be blessed. You will be blessed when you come in and blessed when you go out. I will open the heavens, the storehouse of My bounty, to send rain on your land in season and to bless all the work of your hands. I will make you the head and not the tail. I will grant you abundant prosperity in the land to which I will bring you.

PSALM 132:15; EZEKIEL 34:26; DEUTERONOMY 28

Prayer Declaration

Father, surely You bless the righteous and surround us with Your favor as a shield. I will taste and see, for You are good. Because I fear You and trust You, I will lack nothing. Blessed are those You choose and bring near to live in Your courts, for You fill us with the good things of Your house. You answer us with awesome and righteous deeds. You crown the year with Your bounty, and our carts overflow with abundance.

I AM YOUR PLACE OF SAFETY

MY DAUGHTER, LIE down and sleep in peace, for I will make you to dwell in safety. I will save you with My everlasting salvation, and I will always keep you safe and free from shame. I will search out for My sheep and take care of them. I will rescue you and bring you back from captivity. I will be your shepherd and let you graze on fertile fields, where you will be safe on grassy meadows and green hills. I will bring back the ones who wander off and will bandage those who are hurt. I will protect the ones who are weak.

PSALM 4:8; ISAIAH 48:17; EZEKIEL 34:11–16

Prayer Declaration

I pray to You, Lord! You are my place of safety, and You are my choice in the land of the living. Please answer my prayer. I am completely helpless. Help! They are chasing me, and they are too strong. Rescue me from this prison, so I can praise Your name. And when Your people notice Your wonderful kindness to me, they will rush to my side. You are the Lord of righteousness. I am saved, and I dwell safely.

I WILL TEACH YOU MY WILL

I AM YOUR God, and My Holy Spirit is good. I will lead you in the land of uprightness and teach you to do My will. Whoever does My will is My brother and sister and mother. My love is with those who fear Me, and My righteousness with those who keep My covenant and remember to do My will. How can a young woman stay on the path of purity? By living according to My Word and by seeking Me with all your heart and by not straying from My will. Hide My Word in your heart that you might not sin against Me. Meditate on My precepts and consider My ways.

PSALM 143:10; MATTHEW 12:50;
PSALMS 103:12–13; 119:6–16

Prayer Declaration

Father, You have laid down precepts that are to be fully obeyed. Oh, that my ways were steadfast in obeying your decrees! Then I would not be put to shame when I consider all your commands. I will praise you with an upright heart as I learn your righteous laws. I will obey your decrees. Give me understanding, so that I may keep Your law and obey it with all my heart. Direct me in the path of Your commands, for there I find delight.

I AM YOUR FORTRESS

IF YOU WILL walk righteously and speak uprightly, and stop your ears from hearing of bloodshed, and shut your eyes to avoid looking upon evil, then I will cause you to dwell on the heights. I will be your place of defense in the fortresses of rocks. Bread will be given to you, and water for you will be sure. I will be the strength of My daughters and a fortress of salvation for My anointed ones. I am your rock of refuge to which you can always go. I will save you when you call, for I am your rock and your fortress.

ISAIAH 33:15–16; PSALM 71:3

Prayer Declaration

Lord, You are my steadfast love and my fortress, my high tower and my deliverer, my shield and the One in whom I trust and take refuge, who subdues people under me. I will say of the Lord, "You are my refuge and my fortress, my God, in whom I trust." Whoever fears You has a secure fortress, and You will be a refuge for their children.

MY KINGDOM IS EVERLASTING

MY KINGDOM IS an everlasting kingdom, and My dominion endures through all generations. I am trustworthy in all I promise and faithful in all I do. I have established My throne in heaven, and My kingdom rules over all. Let all speak of the glory of My kingdom and talk of My power. I came to bring in everlasting righteousness and to establish My kingdom. My kingdom is not meat and drink, but righteousness, peace, and joy in the Holy Ghost.

PSALMS 145:11, 13; 103:19; DANIEL 9:24;
ROMANS 14:17

Prayer Declaration

Lord, You have established Your throne in heaven, and Your kingdom rules over all. Your kingdom and reign will touch this generation. You have ransomed me and caused me to enter Your kingdom with singing. You have given me a crown of everlasting joy and gladness, and sorrow and sighing will flee away.

I WILL HEAL THE BROKENHEARTED

I WILL BUILD up Jerusalem and gather the exiles of Israel. I heal the brokenhearted and bind up their wounds. I determine the number of stars and call them each by name. I am mighty in power, and My understanding has no limit. I sustain the humble but cast the wicked to the ground. The righteous call out, and I hear them and deliver them from all their troubles. I am close to the brokenhearted and save those who are crushed in spirit. The righteous woman may have many troubles, but I will deliver her from them all. I will protect her bones; not one of them will be broken.

PSALMS 146:2–6; 34:4–6, 19–20

Prayer Declaration

I will extol You at all times; Your praise will always be on my lips. I will glory in You. When I was afflicted, You heard and made me rejoice. When I sought You, You answered me and delivered me from all my fears. Those who look to You are radiant; their faces are never covered with shame. Your angel encamps around those who fear You, and You deliver them.

I Will Lift Up the Humble

ARISE, MY DAUGHTER, and lift up your hand, for I will not forget the humble. I guide the humble in justice, and I teach the humble My way. I am the God who is enthroned from old. I do not change. I will hear the humble but will humble those who have no fear of Me. I will take delight in My daughters and will crown the humble with victory. Humility is the fear of the Lord, and its wages are riches and honor and life.

PSALMS 10:12; 25:9; 55:19; 149:4; PROVERBS 22:4

Prayer Declaration

Lord, You have heard the desire of the humble; You will prepare their hearts and cause Your ear to hear. You will save the humble but will bring down haughty looks. My soul will make its boast in You. The humble will hear of it and be glad.

I Will Shine My Light on the World

I WILL SEND out My light and My truth and will lead you. It will bring you to My holy hill and to My tabernacle. The day is Mine, and the night also. I have prepared the light and the sun and have set all the borders of the earth. The sun shall no longer be your light by day, nor the brightness of the moon give light to you. For I will be to you an everlasting light and the God of your glory. I am the light of the world. He who follows Me shall not walk in darkness but will have the light of life.

PSALMS 43:3; 74:16–17; ISAIAH 60:19; JOHN 8:12

Prayer Declaration

Where can I go from Your Spirit? Or where can I flee from Your presence? If I ascend into heaven, You are there. If I make my bed in hell, behold, You are there. If I take the wings of the morning and dwell in the uttermost parts of the sea, even there Your hand shall lead me, and Your right hand shall hold me. If I say, "Surely the darkness shall fall on me," even the night shall be light about me; indeed, the darkness shall not hide from You, But the night shines as the day; the darkness and the light are both alike to You.

MY GOVERNMENT WILL NEVER END

FOR UNTO YOU a Child is born, unto you a Son is given; and the government will be upon His shoulder. And His name will be called Wonderful, Counselor, Mighty God, Everlasting Father, Prince of Peace. Of the increase of His government and peace there will be no end, upon the throne of David and over His kingdom, to order it and establish it with judgment and justice from that time forward, even forever.

ISAIAH 9:6–7

Prayer Declaration

Lord, of the increase of Your government and peace there is no end. Let Your government and peace increase from generation to generation.

I WILL GIVE YOU REST

WHEN YOU CROSS over and dwell in the land that I am giving you to inherit, I will give you rest from all your enemies round about, so that you dwell in safety. Then there will be the place where I have chosen to make My name abide. I am the Lord who has given rest to His daughters according to all that I promised. There has not failed one word of all My good promise. Come to Me, all you who labor and are heavy laden, and I will give you rest.

DEUTERONOMY 12:10–11; 1 KINGS 8:56;
MATTHEW 11:28

Prayer Declaration

Let me enter the rest I have in Christ. I have rest from sorrow and from fear and from hard bondage. Let me dwell in a peaceful dwelling place and in a secure home, in an undisturbed place of rest.

MY THRONE IS ESTABLISHED IN MERCY

PRAISE ME AMONG the peoples, and sing to Me among the nations, for My mercy reaches unto the heavens and My truth unto the clouds. My throne is established in mercy, and I sit upon it in truth in the tabernacle of David, judging and seeking justice and hastening righteousness. Sing of My power and sing aloud of My mercy, for I will be your defense and refuge in the day of trouble. My mercy endures forever.

PSALMS 57:9–10; 59:16; ISAIAH 16:5

Prayer Declaration

Because of Your great mercy, I come to Your house, Lord, and I am filled with wonder as I bow down to worship at Your holy temple. Surely goodness and mercy shall follow me all the days of my life, and I will dwell in the house of the Lord forever.

I Will Deliver You From Your Enemies

I AM THE Lord of Zion, and I have been set on the holy hill in power. I rule in the midst of My enemies. Through the greatness of My power, My enemies will submit themselves to Me. All of your hateful enemies will feel like fools, because I will help and comfort you. My plans will happen exactly as I planned. My blueprints will take shape. I will shatter the enemies who trespass on My land and will stomp them into the dirt on My mountains. I will ban them from taking and making slaves of My daughters and will lift the weight of oppression from all shoulders. This is My plan, planned for the whole earth. And it is My hand that will do it, reaching into every nation. God-of-the-Angel-Armies has planned it. Who could ever cancel such plans? My hand has reached out. Who could brush it aside?

PSALMS 66:3; 86:17; ISAIAH 14:24–27, THE MESSAGE

Prayer Declaration

Lead me, O Lord, in Your righteousness because of my enemies. Make my way straight before my face. Because of Your power in me, I can advance against my enemies and scale the walls intended to keep me out. Through You I will do valiantly, for it is You who will tread down my enemies. Let me be delivered out of the hand of my enemies, and let me serve You without fear in holiness and righteousness all the days of my life.

I Am a God of Compassion

THE HEAVENS SHOUT for joy, and the earth rejoices. The mountains burst into song, for I comfort My people and will have compassion on My afflicted ones. I will comfort My church and look with compassion on all her ruins. I will make all My goodness pass before you, and I will proclaim My name before you. I will be gracious to whom I will be gracious, and I will have compassion on whom I will have compassion. I am a God full of compassion, and gracious, long-suffering, and abundant in mercy and truth.

ISAIAH 49:13; 51:3; EXODUS 33:19; PSALM 86:15

Prayer Declaration

Lord, You have redeemed my life from the pit and have crowned me with love and compassion. You long to be gracious to me. You rise to show me compassion. You are a God of justice. I will wait for You and be blessed. Through Your mercies we are not consumed, and Your compassions fail not.

I HAVE GIVEN YOU MY WISDOM

LET ALL THE people, all the inhabitants of the world, give ear and hear My wisdom. Let them hear and understand My parables of the kingdom. I will give you the spirit of wisdom and revelation in My knowledge, and I will let the eyes of your understanding be enlightened to know the hope of My calling and the riches of the glory of My inheritance. I store up sound wisdom for the upright and am a shield to those who walk uprightly. I will teach you in the way of wisdom and will lead you in right paths.

PSALM 49:1–4; EPHESIANS 1:17–18;
PROVERBS 2:7; 4:11

Prayer Declaration

Let wisdom and knowledge be my stability and strength of salvation, and the fear of the Lord my treasure. You have filled me with Your Spirit, in wisdom and understanding, in knowledge and all manner of workmanship. Happy are Your daughters who stand continually before You and hear Your wisdom.

I AM YOUR REDEEMER

I WILL REDEEM you out of all your troubles. I redeem the souls of My daughters, and none of those who trust in Me shall be condemned. I will redeem your life from oppression and violence. Precious will be your blood in My sight. I am your mighty Redeemer, and I will plead your cause against your enemies. Fear not, for I have redeemed you. I have called you by your name; you are Mine. When you pass through the water, I will be with you; and through the rivers, they shall not overflow you. When you walk through the fire, you shall not be burned, nor shall the flame scorch you. For I am the Lord your God, the Holy One of Israel, your Savior; I gave My Son for your ransom.

PSALMS 25:22; 34:22; PROVERBS 23:11; PSALM 43:1–3

Prayer Declaration

*Let the words of my mouth and the meditation of my heart
be acceptable in Your sight, O Lord, my strength and my
Redeemer. I know that my Redeemer lives, and He shall
stand at last on the earth. My lips shall greatly rejoice when
I sing to You, and my soul, which You have redeemed.*

I Sent My Son to Save the World

I SENT My Son into the world to be lifted up, that whoever believes in Him should not perish but have eternal life. For I so loved the world that I gave My only begotten Son, that whoever believes in Him should not perish but have everlasting life. For I did not send My Son into the world to condemn the world, but that the world through Him might be saved. For the wages of sin is death, but the gift of God is eternal life in Christ Jesus your Lord. For by grace you have been saved through faith, and that not of yourself; it is the gift of God!

JOHN 3:15–17; ROMANS 6:23

Prayer Declaration

Father, thanks be to You for Your indescribable gift!

I WILL FILL YOU WITH JOY AND GLADNESS

I WILL CAUSE your desert places to be like the Garden of Eden, and your wastelands like My garden. I will fill you with joy, gladness, thanksgiving, and the sound of singing. I have ransomed you, My daughter, and caused you to enter Zion with singing. I have given you a crown of everlasting joy and gladness, and sorrow and sighing will flee away. My light is sown for the righteous, and My gladness for the upright in heart. I am the Lord your God, and I am in your midst; I will rejoice over you with gladness. I will quiet you with My love and will rejoice over you with singing.

ISAIAH 51:3, 11; PSALM 97:11; ZEPHANIAH 3:17

Prayer Declaration

Father, in You I will obtain joy and gladness, and sorrow and sighing will flee from my life. Before You are honor and majesty; strength and gladness are in Your dwelling. You have turned my mourning into dancing; You have put off my sackcloth and clothed me with gladness.

GOD IS THE FULFILLMENT OF MY LIFE

I Will Make the Crooked Straight

I will comfort you, My daughter, for your warfare is ended and your iniquity is pardoned. You have received from Me double for all your sins. Every valley will be exalted, and every mountain and hill brought low. The crooked places shall be made straight and the crooked places smooth. My glory will be revealed, and all flesh will see it together. I will feed My flock like a shepherd and will gather the lambs with My arm. I will carry them in My bosom and gently lead those who are with young.

Isaiah 40:1–5, 11

Prayer Declaration

Have you not known? Have you not heard? The everlasting God,
the Lord, the Creator of the ends of the earth, neither faints nor
is weary. His understanding is unsearchable. He gives power to
the weak, and to those who have no might He increases strength.
Even the youths shall faint and be weary, and the young men
shall utterly fall. But those who wait on the Lord shall renew
their strength; they shall mount up with wings like eagles; they
shall run and not be weary; they shall walk and not faint.

I WILL RENEW YOUR STRENGTH

I WILL SATISFY your desires with good things, so that your youth is renewed like the eagle's. I send forth My Spirit and renew the face of the earth. Therefore do not lose heart, My daughter. Even though your outward man is perishing, yet the inward man is being renewed day by day. For your light affliction, which is but for a moment, is working for you a far more exceeding and eternal weight of glory. Do not look on the things that are seen, but at the things that are not seen. For the things that are seen are temporary, but the things that are not seen are eternal.

PSALMS 103:5; 104:30; 2 CORINTHIANS 4:16–18

Prayer Declaration

I will wait upon the Lord and renew my strength. Create in me a clean heart, O God, and renew a steadfast spirit within me. He who raised up the Lord Jesus will also raise me up with Jesus and will present me before Your face.

I Will Take Away Your Fear

I AM YOUR light and your salvation; whom shall you fear? I am the strength of your life; of whom shall you be afraid? You will enjoy the rest you have in Me, for you will rest from sorrow and from fear and from hard bondage. Wisdom and knowledge will be your stability, and My strength will be your salvation. The fear of the Lord is your treasure. I will establish you in righteousness, and tyranny will be far from you. You have nothing to fear, for terror will be removed and will not come near you.

PSALM 27:1; ISAIAH 14:3; 33:6; 54:14

Prayer Declaration

Lord, I will not fear, for You are with me. You will strengthen me, help me, and uphold you with Your righteous right hand. I will not fear, for You, Lord, will hold my hand and help me. Let Your mercy be upon those who fear You from generation to generation.

I Have a Glorious Future for You

For I know the thoughts that I think toward you, thoughts of peace and not of evil, to give you a future and a hope. There is hope in your future that your children shall come back to their own border. It shall come to pass in the latter days that the mountain of the Lord's house shall be established on the top of the mountains and shall be exalted above the hills, and peoples shall flow to it. Many nations shall come and say, "Come, and let us go up to the mountain of the Lord, to the house of the God of Jacob; He will teach us His ways, and we shall walk in His paths."

JEREMIAH 29:11; 31:17; MICAH 4:1–2

Prayer Declaration

You, Lord, are all I want! You are my choice, and You keep me safe. You make my life pleasant, and my future is bright. You will judge between many peoples and rebuke strong nations afar off. They shall beat their swords into plowshares and their spears into pruning hooks. Nation shall not lift up sword against nation, neither shall they learn war anymore. All people will walk in Your name forever and ever.

I Have Given You New Life

You are buried with Christ through baptism into death, that just as Christ was raised from the dead by My glory, even so should you walk in newness of life. For if you have been united together in the likeness of His death, certainly you shall also be in the likeness of His resurrection. Behold, the former things have come to pass, and new things I declare; behold, they spring forth. I will open rivers in desolate heights and fountains in the midst of the valleys. I will make the wilderness a pool of water and the dry land springs of water. Fear not, for I am with you, My daughter; be not dismayed, for I am your God. I will strengthen you, yes, I will help you. I will uphold you with My righteous right hand.

Romans 6:4–5; Isaiah 41:10, 18

Prayer Declaration

You have put a new song in my mouth, and I sing praises to You. Many will see Your goodness and will fear and trust in Your name. I will proclaim the good news of righteousness in the great assembly; indeed, I will not restrain my lips.

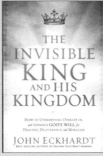
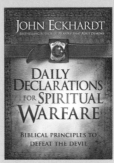

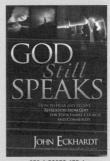